Moving to Bulgaria

A guide for prospective expatriate

By Alex Bugeja

Created using the Qyx AI Book Creator

See "About this book" in the Introduction

Table of Contents

Introduction

Introduction

Bulgaria, nestled in the heart of the Balkan Peninsula, is a country of captivating beauty, rich history, and vibrant culture. With its stunning mountain ranges, picturesque coastlines, and charming villages, Bulgaria offers a unique and enticing lifestyle for those seeking a change of pace. In recent years, Bulgaria has become an increasingly popular destination for expatriates from all over the world, drawn by its affordability, welcoming atmosphere, and the opportunity to experience a different way of life.

This book is your comprehensive guide to moving to Bulgaria, specifically tailored for prospective expatriates. We understand that relocating to a new country can be both exciting and daunting, and our aim is to provide you with the essential information and practical advice you need to make your move as smooth and successful as possible.

Throughout this book, you'll find chapters dedicated to every aspect of expat life in Bulgaria. From navigating the visa and residency requirements to finding the perfect home, understanding the healthcare system, and exploring job opportunities, we've got you covered. We'll also delve into the intricacies of Bulgarian culture and etiquette, helping you to seamlessly integrate into your new community.

This book is not about general moving advice that could apply to any overseas destination. Instead, we focus exclusively on the specific nuances of moving to Bulgaria. We'll share insights into the local customs, traditions, and social norms that will help you avoid common pitfalls and embrace the Bulgarian way of life. We'll also provide you with practical tips and resources to help you settle in and make the most of your Bulgarian experience.

Whether you're dreaming of a peaceful retirement in the countryside, seeking new career opportunities, or simply yearning for an adventure in a new land, this book will equip you with the knowledge and confidence to make your move to Bulgaria a resounding success. Let's begin your journey!

About this book

The author, Dr Alex Bugeja is the Founder & CEO of Traffikoo, a Texas company specializing in online advertising, AI tools, and SaaS solutions. He is originally from Malta and now lives in Texas.

This book was created in part using the Qyx AI Book Creator, a project developed and maintained by Traffikoo. Qyx AI Book Creator is a powerful and affordable AI ghostwriter, capable of creating entire books on virtually any subject. It is suitable for prospective authors who wish to create books to sell to others, for subject matter experts writing books to position themselves as thought leaders in their fields, and for just creating books for personal use. Qyx AI Book Creator books are perfectly useable as is, or as drafts for those wishing to add their own personal touch.

Besides serving as a guide to moving to Bulgaria, we hope this book also inspires you to try out Qyx AI Book Creator for yourself.

CHAPTER ONE: Visa and Residency Requirements: Navigating Bulgarian Bureaucracy

Moving to Bulgaria, like relocating to any other country, involves a fair share of paperwork and administrative processes. While it might seem daunting initially, understanding the visa and residency requirements is crucial for a smooth transition. This chapter provides a detailed guide to navigating the Bulgarian bureaucracy, ensuring you have the correct documentation to live and work in this beautiful Balkan nation.

Short-Term Visas: Exploring Bulgaria for a Limited Period

If you're planning a short visit to Bulgaria, perhaps for tourism or business, you might need a short-term visa. Citizens of most European Union countries, as well as several other nations, can enter Bulgaria visa-free for up to 90 days within a 180-day period. However, it's essential to check the specific visa requirements based on your nationality before you travel.

For those requiring a short-term visa, the process typically involves applying at a Bulgarian embassy or consulate in your home country. You'll need to provide supporting documents like a valid passport, travel itinerary, proof of accommodation, and financial means. The visa processing time can vary, so it's best to apply well in advance of your intended travel date.

Long-Term Visas and Residency: Staying in Bulgaria for Extended Periods

If you're looking to stay in Bulgaria for an extended period, exceeding the 90-day limit allowed by a short-term visa, you'll need to obtain a long-term visa or residency permit. Bulgaria offers various types of long-term visas, each catering to specific purposes like work, study, or family reunification.

Work Visa (Type D): Employment Opportunities in Bulgaria

For individuals seeking employment in Bulgaria, a work visa (Type D) is mandatory. The application process usually requires a pre-approved work permit from a Bulgarian employer. The employer initiates the work permit application on your behalf, demonstrating that they couldn't find a suitable candidate from within the EU or EEA. Once the work permit is granted, you can apply for a work visa at a Bulgarian embassy or consulate.

The required documents typically include a valid passport, employment contract, educational and professional qualifications, and a medical certificate. The work visa is usually issued for one year, allowing you to live and work in Bulgaria. You can apply for renewal before its expiry, provided your employment continues.

Long-Term Residence Permit: Establishing a Permanent Base in Bulgaria

A long-term residence permit allows you to live in Bulgaria for an extended period, typically five years, with the possibility of renewal. This permit grants you similar rights to Bulgarian citizens, excluding the right to vote. There are several grounds for obtaining a long-term residence permit, including:

- **Employment:** If you've been working in Bulgaria on a work visa (Type D) for at least five years, you can apply for a long-term residence permit.

- **Investment:** Foreign investors who meet certain criteria, such as investing a significant amount in a Bulgarian business or real estate, can qualify for a long-term residence permit.

- **Family Reunification:** If you're married to a Bulgarian citizen or a foreigner with a long-term residence permit, you can apply for family reunification.

- **Study:** Students enrolled in accredited Bulgarian universities for long-term courses can also apply for a residence permit for the duration of their studies.

The application process for a long-term residence permit involves submitting a comprehensive set of documents, including a valid passport, proof of accommodation, health insurance, financial means, and, depending on the basis of your application, additional documentation like marriage certificates, investment proof, or university enrollment confirmations.

Permanent Residence: Making Bulgaria Your Home

After five years of continuous legal residence in Bulgaria with a long-term residence permit, you become eligible to apply for permanent residence. Permanent residence grants you indefinite permission to live and work in Bulgaria, offering greater stability and security. The application process requires you to demonstrate your integration into Bulgarian society, which might include language proficiency, stable income, and a clean criminal record.

Navigating the Application Process: Tips for Success

The Bulgarian bureaucracy can be complex, and navigating the visa and residency application processes requires patience and meticulous attention to detail. Here are some tips to enhance your chances of success:

- **Start Early:** The application process can take time, so starting early is crucial. Research the specific requirements well in advance of your intended travel or relocation date.

- **Gather All Necessary Documents:** Ensure you have all the required documents, including translated and notarized copies where applicable. Check the official websites of the Bulgarian Ministry of Foreign Affairs or the embassy for the most up-to-date information.

- **Be Accurate and Consistent:** Provide accurate and consistent information in your application and supporting documents. Any discrepancies can lead to delays or rejection.

- **Seek Professional Assistance:** If you find the process overwhelming, consider seeking professional assistance from immigration lawyers or consultants. They can guide you through the steps and ensure your application meets all the requirements.

Staying Informed: Keeping Up with Changes in Regulations

Bulgarian immigration laws and regulations can change, so staying informed is essential. Regularly check the official websites of the Bulgarian Ministry of Foreign Affairs and the embassy or consulate for any updates or modifications to the visa and residency requirements.

CHAPTER TWO: Finding Your Perfect Home: Exploring Bulgaria's Diverse Housing Options

Once you've navigated the visa and residency requirements, the next crucial step in your Bulgarian adventure is finding a place to call home. Bulgaria offers a diverse range of housing options, from modern apartments in bustling cities to charming houses in tranquil villages, catering to various tastes and budgets. This chapter delves into the intricacies of the Bulgarian housing market, providing you with the insights and guidance you need to find the perfect dwelling that suits your lifestyle and preferences.

City Living: Embracing the Urban Vibe

Bulgaria's cities offer a dynamic blend of modern amenities, cultural attractions, and historical charm. If you thrive in a fast-paced environment with easy access to entertainment, shopping, and nightlife, city living might be the ideal choice for you.

Sofia: The Cosmopolitan Capital

Sofia, the capital city, is a vibrant metropolis brimming with history, culture, and a cosmopolitan atmosphere. It's home to a wide array of housing options, from stylish apartments in the city center to spacious houses in the more tranquil suburbs.

The city center, with its iconic landmarks, bustling squares, and vibrant nightlife, attracts those seeking a lively urban experience. Modern apartment complexes with amenities like swimming pools, gyms, and underground parking are increasingly popular, offering a comfortable and convenient lifestyle. The suburbs, on the other hand, provide a more relaxed setting, often with larger houses and gardens, appealing to families and those seeking a quieter pace.

Plovdiv: The Ancient Cultural Hub

Plovdiv, Bulgaria's second-largest city, is an ancient cultural hub with a rich history spanning millennia. Its charming old town, with its cobblestone streets, traditional houses, and Roman ruins, exudes an undeniable charm.

Plovdiv offers a mix of housing options, from renovated apartments in historical buildings to modern complexes in the newer parts of the city. Living in the old town immerses you in Plovdiv's unique atmosphere, while the newer districts provide a more contemporary lifestyle.

Varna: The Coastal Gem

Varna, a major port city on the Black Sea coast, is known for its beautiful beaches, bustling promenade, and lively summer atmosphere. It's a popular destination for both tourists and expats seeking a coastal lifestyle.

Varna's housing market offers a diverse range of choices, from seafront apartments with breathtaking views to detached houses in the quieter suburbs. The city center and the areas surrounding the main beach are prime locations for those seeking proximity to the coast and its attractions.

Rural Retreats: Embracing Tranquility and Nature

If you crave a slower pace of life, surrounded by nature's tranquility, Bulgaria's rural areas offer an idyllic escape. With their picturesque villages, rolling hills, and stunning mountain vistas, rural retreats provide a unique opportunity to reconnect with nature and experience a more traditional Bulgarian lifestyle.

Mountain Villages: Breathtaking Vistas and Outdoor Adventures

Bulgaria's mountain ranges, with their towering peaks, verdant forests, and charming villages, are a haven for nature lovers and outdoor enthusiasts. Living in a mountain village offers a serene and picturesque setting, with ample opportunities for hiking, skiing, and exploring the breathtaking natural landscapes.

Many mountain villages feature traditional Bulgarian houses, often built from stone and wood, exuding a rustic charm. Renovated houses with modern amenities offer a comfortable blend of traditional aesthetics and contemporary comfort.

Coastal Villages: Sun, Sand, and a Relaxed Vibe

Bulgaria's Black Sea coastline boasts numerous charming villages, each with its unique character and appeal. Living in a coastal village provides easy access to the beach, a relaxed atmosphere, and the opportunity to enjoy the Mediterranean climate.

Coastal villages offer a mix of housing options, from traditional fishermen's houses to modern apartments and villas. Seafront properties are highly sought after, offering stunning views and a prime location for those seeking a coastal lifestyle.

Types of Housing: Finding the Right Fit

Bulgaria's housing market offers a wide variety of property types, each with its advantages and considerations. Understanding the different types of housing can help you narrow down your search and find the dwelling that best suits your needs and preferences.

Apartments: Modern Living and Convenience

Apartments are a popular choice for both city dwellers and those seeking a low-maintenance lifestyle. They come in various sizes and configurations, from cozy studios to spacious multi-bedroom units.

Modern apartment complexes often feature amenities like swimming pools, gyms, and secure parking, offering a comfortable and convenient lifestyle. Older apartment buildings, while lacking these amenities, might offer more affordable options and a unique architectural charm.

Houses: Space, Privacy, and Outdoor Living

Houses provide more space, privacy, and the opportunity for outdoor living. They range from traditional Bulgarian houses with courtyards to modern villas with gardens and swimming pools.

Detached houses offer the utmost privacy and independence, while semi-detached and terraced houses provide a sense of community and shared outdoor spaces. Houses typically require more maintenance than apartments, but offer the advantage of owning a piece of land.

Rural Properties: Land, Farming, and a Connection to Nature

Rural properties, encompassing houses, farmhouses, and land, offer a unique opportunity to connect with nature and embrace a more self-sufficient lifestyle. They range from small plots of land with basic dwellings to large farms with extensive acreage.

Rural properties are ideal for those seeking a peaceful and secluded lifestyle, with the possibility of growing their own food, keeping livestock, or developing a smallholding. However, they might require more self-reliance and a willingness to adapt to a rural way of life.

Buying or Renting: Making the Right Choice

Deciding whether to buy or rent a property in Bulgaria depends on your individual circumstances, financial situation, and long-term plans. Both options have their pros and cons, and carefully considering your needs and preferences is crucial before making a decision.

Buying a Property: Long-Term Investment and Ownership

Buying a property in Bulgaria can be a sound investment, offering the security of ownership and the potential for capital appreciation. It's an ideal choice for those seeking a permanent base in Bulgaria and are financially prepared for the initial outlay and ongoing costs associated with property ownership.

The process of buying a property in Bulgaria typically involves engaging a reputable real estate agent, finding a suitable property, negotiating the price, conducting due diligence, securing financing if required, and finalizing the purchase through a notary. It's essential to understand the legal and financial aspects of property ownership in Bulgaria and seek professional advice throughout the process.

Renting a Property: Flexibility and Lower Initial Costs

Renting a property in Bulgaria offers greater flexibility and lower initial costs compared to buying. It's an excellent option for those who are new to the country, are unsure about their long-term plans, or prefer not to commit to property ownership.

The rental market in Bulgaria offers a wide range of choices, from short-term rentals for a few months to long-term leases for a year or more. Rental agreements typically outline the terms and conditions, including rent payment, deposit, and responsibilities for maintenance.

Finding Your Perfect Home: Tips and Resources

Finding the perfect home in Bulgaria requires research, patience, and a clear understanding of your needs and preferences. Here are some tips and resources to help you navigate the Bulgarian housing market:

Research and Define Your Criteria

Before embarking on your house hunt, take the time to research different areas, property types, and price ranges. Consider your lifestyle, budget, and long-term plans. Define your must-have features, such as number of bedrooms, proximity to amenities, or outdoor space.

Engage a Reputable Real Estate Agent

A reliable real estate agent can be invaluable in your property search. They have local market knowledge, access to a wide range of properties, and can guide you through the buying or renting process. Choose an agent with a good reputation and experience working with expats.

Explore Online Property Portals

Online property portals provide a convenient way to browse available properties, filter by criteria, and get an idea of market prices. Popular portals in Bulgaria include imot.bg, olx.bg, and alo.bg.

Network and Ask for Recommendations

Talk to other expats, locals, and colleagues for recommendations and insights into different neighborhoods and housing options. Networking can often lead to hidden gems and valuable information that might not be readily available online.

Visit Properties and Get a Feel for the Area

Once you've shortlisted potential properties, schedule viewings to get a feel for the space, the surrounding area, and the overall vibe. Pay attention to details, ask questions, and trust your instincts.

Negotiate the Price and Terms

Whether buying or renting, be prepared to negotiate the price and terms of the agreement. Research comparable properties in the area to gauge fair market value and don't hesitate to counter-offer.

Understand the Legal and Financial Aspects

Buying or renting a property in Bulgaria involves legal and financial considerations. Familiarize yourself with the relevant laws, regulations, and tax implications. Seek professional advice from a lawyer and financial advisor to ensure a smooth and secure transaction.

CHAPTER THREE: Healthcare in Bulgaria: Understanding the System and Finding a Doctor

Transitioning to a new healthcare system in a foreign country can be a significant concern for expats. This chapter aims to demystify the Bulgarian healthcare system, shedding light on its structure, accessibility, and the steps involved in finding a doctor and receiving medical care. Understanding these aspects can alleviate anxiety and empower you to navigate the Bulgarian healthcare landscape confidently.

The Bulgarian Healthcare System: A Blend of Public and Private

Bulgaria's healthcare system is a two-tiered structure, encompassing both public and private sectors. The public system, funded through mandatory health insurance contributions, provides universal healthcare coverage to all Bulgarian citizens and legally residing foreigners. The private sector, while smaller, offers an alternative for those seeking faster access to specialized treatments or a higher level of comfort and amenities.

National Health Insurance Fund (NHIF): The Backbone of Public Healthcare

The National Health Insurance Fund (NHIF) is the primary institution responsible for managing and financing public healthcare in Bulgaria. It collects mandatory health insurance contributions from employed individuals, self-employed persons, and pensioners, pooling these funds to cover the costs of medical services for insured individuals.

Health Insurance Card: Your Gateway to Public Healthcare

To access public healthcare services in Bulgaria, you'll need a health insurance card issued by the NHIF. If you're employed, your employer will typically handle the registration process and deductions for health insurance contributions. Self-employed individuals and those not covered by employer contributions are responsible for registering with the NHIF and making their own payments.

Your health insurance card entitles you to a range of medical services, including consultations with general practitioners (GPs), specialists, hospitalization, emergency care, and prescribed medications. However, it's important to note that the public healthcare system often involves waiting lists for certain procedures or specialist appointments. Additionally, co-payments might apply for some services or medications.

Private Health Insurance: An Alternative for Faster Access and Comfort

Private health insurance offers an alternative to the public system, providing faster access to specialized treatments, shorter waiting times, and a wider choice of hospitals and doctors. Private clinics and hospitals often offer a higher level of comfort and amenities, appealing to those seeking a more personalized healthcare experience.

Numerous private health insurance providers operate in Bulgaria, offering various plans and coverage options. The cost of private health insurance premiums varies depending on factors like age, health status, and the extent of coverage. It's essential to carefully compare plans and choose one that aligns with your healthcare needs and budget.

Finding a Doctor: Navigating the Options

Whether you opt for public or private healthcare, finding a doctor who meets your needs is essential for your well-being in Bulgaria. Here are some ways to navigate the options and find a suitable healthcare provider:

General Practitioners (GPs): Your First Point of Contact

General practitioners (GPs) are your primary healthcare providers, offering routine checkups, diagnoses, and referrals to specialists if needed. In the public healthcare system, you'll typically be assigned a GP based on your address. You can find information about GPs in your area on the NHIF website or by inquiring at your local municipality.

In the private sector, you have more flexibility in choosing a GP. You can ask for recommendations from other expats, consult online directories of private clinics, or contact your private health insurance provider for a list of affiliated GPs.

Specialists: Seeking Expert Medical Care

If you require specialized medical care, your GP can refer you to a specialist in the public healthcare system. However, waiting times for specialist appointments can be lengthy. Private health insurance often provides faster access to specialists, allowing you to choose from a wider range of providers.

You can find information about specialists in Bulgaria through online directories, professional medical associations, or by asking for recommendations from your GP or private health insurance provider.

Hospitals: Public and Private Options

Bulgaria has a network of public hospitals providing a range of medical services, including emergency care, surgery, and specialized treatments. Public hospitals are often overcrowded and might lack the comfort and amenities found in private facilities.

Private hospitals, while more expensive, offer a higher level of care, modern equipment, and shorter waiting times. Many private hospitals cater to international patients, providing multilingual staff and services tailored to expats' needs.

Communicating with Your Doctor: Overcoming Language Barriers

Communicating effectively with your doctor is crucial for receiving appropriate medical care. While many healthcare professionals in larger cities and private clinics speak English, you might encounter language barriers in smaller towns or rural areas.

To overcome language challenges, consider the following:

Learn Basic Bulgarian Medical Terms

Familiarizing yourself with basic Bulgarian medical terms can be helpful when communicating with doctors and pharmacists. Simple phrases like "I have a headache," "I need a prescription," or "Where is the nearest hospital?" can make a significant difference in ensuring you receive the necessary care.

Bring a Bulgarian-Speaking Friend or Interpreter

If you're not confident in your Bulgarian language skills, consider bringing a Bulgarian-speaking friend or hiring a professional interpreter to accompany you to medical appointments. They can facilitate communication and ensure you understand your doctor's instructions and diagnoses.

Use Translation Apps or Dictionaries

Smartphone translation apps and online dictionaries can be useful tools for bridging the language gap. However, it's essential to exercise caution when relying solely on machine translations, as they might not always be accurate, especially for complex medical terminology.

Seek Out English-Speaking Doctors or Clinics

In larger cities and tourist areas, you can often find English-speaking doctors or clinics specializing in expat healthcare. Online directories and expat forums can be helpful resources for identifying these providers.

Pharmacies: Accessing Medications and Over-the-Counter Remedies

Pharmacies (аптека - apteka) in Bulgaria are readily available, offering a wide range of prescription and over-the-counter medications. You'll need a doctor's prescription to purchase most medications, but some over-the-counter remedies like pain relievers, cold medicine, and vitamins are available without a prescription.

Pharmacists in Bulgaria are knowledgeable and can often provide advice on common ailments and over-the-counter remedies. They can also clarify dosage instructions and potential side effects of medications.

Emergency Medical Services: When to Seek Immediate Care

In case of a medical emergency, dial 112, the pan-European emergency number, to access ambulance services and immediate medical assistance. Bulgaria has a network of emergency medical services, including ambulance crews, emergency rooms, and specialized medical teams.

When calling emergency services, be prepared to provide your location, a brief description of the situation, and any relevant medical information. If you're not fluent in Bulgarian, try to find someone who can communicate with the emergency dispatcher on your behalf.

Health Tips for Expats: Staying Healthy in Bulgaria

Maintaining good health is essential for enjoying your expat experience in Bulgaria. Here are some health tips to keep in mind:

Stay Up-to-Date on Vaccinations

Before traveling to Bulgaria, consult your doctor about recommended vaccinations. Ensure your routine vaccinations, like tetanus, diphtheria, and measles, are up-to-date. You might also consider vaccinations for hepatitis A and B, rabies, and tick-borne encephalitis, depending on your travel plans and activities.

Drink Bottled Water

While tap water in Bulgaria is generally safe to drink, many expats prefer to err on the side of caution and consume bottled water, especially when first arriving in the country. Bottled water is readily available in supermarkets, convenience stores, and restaurants.

Be Mindful of Food Safety

Bulgarian cuisine is delicious and diverse, but it's essential to be mindful of food safety, especially when eating street food or at small, local restaurants. Ensure food is properly cooked, avoid raw or undercooked meat and seafood, and wash fruits and vegetables thoroughly before consumption.

Protect Yourself from Ticks

Ticks are prevalent in Bulgaria, especially in wooded areas and during warmer months. Wear long sleeves and pants when hiking or spending time outdoors, use insect repellent containing DEET, and check your body for ticks after outdoor activities. If you find a tick, remove it promptly using tweezers, pulling it straight out without twisting or crushing it.

Stay Active and Enjoy the Outdoors

Bulgaria offers a wealth of opportunities for outdoor activities, from hiking and skiing in the mountains to swimming and sunbathing on the Black Sea coast. Staying active and enjoying the outdoors can contribute to your physical and mental well-being.

Embrace a Healthy Lifestyle

Maintaining a healthy lifestyle, including a balanced diet, regular exercise, and sufficient sleep, is crucial for overall well-being. Embrace the Mediterranean diet, rich in fruits, vegetables, and olive oil, and enjoy the abundance of fresh produce available in Bulgarian markets.

CHAPTER FOUR: Education for Expats: Schools, Universities, and Language Learning

Whether you're moving to Bulgaria with your family or seeking to expand your own educational horizons, understanding the educational landscape is essential. This chapter explores the various educational options available to expats in Bulgaria, from preschools and primary schools to universities and language learning institutions. We'll delve into the intricacies of the Bulgarian education system, providing you with insights and guidance to make informed choices for yourself and your family.

Early Childhood Education: Nurturing Young Minds

Bulgaria offers a range of preschool options for children aged 3 to 6, providing a foundation for their educational journey. These institutions, known as детска градина (detska gradina), offer a nurturing environment where children engage in play-based learning, develop social skills, and prepare for primary school.

Public Kindergartens: Affordable and Accessible

Public kindergartens are widely available throughout Bulgaria, offering an affordable and accessible option for families. They follow the national curriculum, providing a structured learning environment with a focus on language development, early literacy, numeracy, and creative arts.

Enrollment in public kindergartens typically begins in the spring, with priority given to children living in the catchment area. Fees are generally low, covering basic expenses like meals and materials.

Private Kindergartens: Diverse Options and Specialized Programs

Private kindergartens offer a diverse range of educational approaches, philosophies, and specialized programs. They often have smaller class sizes, more personalized attention, and a wider range of extracurricular activities.

Some private kindergartens follow international curricula, such as the Montessori or Waldorf approach, while others focus on specific areas like language immersion or early childhood development. Fees for private kindergartens vary depending on the institution, location, and program offerings.

Primary and Secondary Education: Navigating the School System

Bulgaria's compulsory education system spans 12 years, divided into primary (grades 1-8) and secondary (grades 9-12) levels. Public schools are free and follow the national curriculum, providing a comprehensive education encompassing core subjects like Bulgarian language and literature, mathematics, science, history, and foreign languages.

Public Schools: The Core of the Education System

Public schools are the backbone of Bulgaria's education system, offering a solid foundation in core subjects and preparing students for higher education or vocational training. They are widely accessible, with a school in almost every town and village.

Enrollment in public schools is based on catchment areas, with priority given to children living within the designated zone. While public schools are free, parents might contribute to additional expenses like textbooks, school supplies, and extracurricular activities.

Private Schools: Alternative Options and Specialized Programs

Private schools offer an alternative to the public system, often with smaller class sizes, a more personalized approach, and a wider range of extracurricular activities. They might follow international curricula, such as the International Baccalaureate (IB) or the British system, or specialize in areas like languages, arts, or sports.

Fees for private schools vary depending on the institution, location, and program offerings. Some private schools offer scholarships or financial aid to deserving students.

Choosing the Right School: Factors to Consider

Selecting the right school for your child is a significant decision, and several factors come into play. Consider the following:

- **Location:** Choose a school within a reasonable distance from your home, considering transportation options and commute times.

- **Curriculum:** Decide whether you prefer a school following the national curriculum or an international one, based on your child's educational background and future aspirations.

- **Language of Instruction:** If your child is not fluent in Bulgarian, consider schools offering bilingual programs or English-language instruction.

- **Class Size and Teacher-Student Ratio:** Smaller class sizes and a lower teacher-student ratio can provide more individualized attention and support.

- **Extracurricular Activities:** Explore the school's extracurricular offerings, such as sports, arts, music, or clubs, to align with your child's interests and talents.

- **Reputation and Academic Performance:** Research the school's reputation, academic performance, and student outcomes to gauge its overall quality.

- **Fees and Costs:** Factor in the school's fees and any additional expenses, such as textbooks, uniforms, or extracurricular activities, to ensure it fits your budget.

Schooling for Expat Children: Unique Considerations

Expat children face unique challenges when integrating into a new school system, particularly regarding language barriers and cultural differences. Here are some considerations:

- **Language Support:** Ensure the school provides adequate language support for non-Bulgarian speaking students, such as language classes, tutoring, or bilingual programs.

- **Cultural Sensitivity:** Choose a school with a welcoming and inclusive environment, sensitive to cultural differences and supportive of expat students' needs.

- **Transition Programs:** Inquire about transition programs or orientation sessions designed to help expat children adjust to the new school and make friends.

- **Extracurricular Activities:** Encourage your child to participate in extracurricular activities to make friends, develop interests, and integrate into the school community.

Higher Education: Universities and Vocational Training

Bulgaria boasts a long tradition of higher education, with numerous universities and institutions offering a wide range of academic and vocational programs. Whether you're seeking a bachelor's degree, a master's program, or specialized training, Bulgaria's higher education system provides diverse options.

Universities: Academic Excellence and Research Opportunities

Bulgaria has several public and private universities, offering undergraduate and postgraduate programs in various disciplines, including humanities, social sciences, natural sciences, engineering, medicine, and business. Public universities are generally more affordable than private ones, with tuition fees determined by the program and the student's nationality.

Sofia University "St. Kliment Ohridski," the oldest and most prestigious university in Bulgaria, enjoys a strong reputation for academic excellence and research. Other prominent universities include the Technical University of Sofia, the University of Plovdiv "Paisii Hilendarski," and the Medical University of Sofia.

Admission Requirements: Navigating the Application Process

Admission requirements for Bulgarian universities vary depending on the institution and program. Generally, you'll need to provide:

- **High School Diploma or Equivalent:** A certified copy of your high school diploma or equivalent qualification, translated into Bulgarian and legalized.

- **Academic Transcripts:** Official transcripts of your previous academic records, translated into Bulgarian and legalized.

- **Language Proficiency:** Proof of proficiency in Bulgarian, typically through a language certificate or an entrance exam. Some universities offer programs taught in English, requiring proof of English language proficiency.

- **Entrance Exam:** Some programs might require you to take an entrance exam, assessing your knowledge in specific subjects related to your chosen field of study.

- **Application Fee:** A non-refundable application fee, payable to the university.

Vocational Training: Practical Skills and Career Pathways

Vocational training institutions, known as професионални гимназии (profesionalni gimnazii), offer specialized programs in various trades and professions, providing students with practical skills and a direct pathway to employment. These programs typically last three to four years, combining theoretical instruction with hands-on training.

Vocational training covers diverse fields, including tourism, hospitality, culinary arts, automotive mechanics, construction, hairdressing, and beauty therapy. Graduates receive a certificate or diploma, recognized by the Bulgarian government and relevant professional associations.

Language Learning: Mastering Bulgarian for Integration

Learning Bulgarian is highly beneficial for expats, facilitating communication, cultural integration, and access to a wider range of opportunities. While English is spoken in larger cities and tourist areas, fluency in Bulgarian opens doors to deeper connections with locals, a better understanding of Bulgarian culture, and a more fulfilling expat experience.

Language Schools: Structured Courses and Immersion Programs

Numerous language schools operate in Bulgaria, offering structured Bulgarian language courses for all levels, from beginners to advanced learners. These courses typically focus on grammar, vocabulary, pronunciation, and conversational skills.

Some language schools also offer immersion programs, where students live with Bulgarian families, attend language classes, and participate in cultural activities, providing a comprehensive and immersive learning experience.

Private Tutors: Personalized Instruction and Flexible Scheduling

Private tutors offer personalized language instruction tailored to your individual needs and learning style. They can provide one-on-one lessons, focusing on specific areas like grammar, pronunciation, or conversational practice.

Private tutors offer flexible scheduling, accommodating your availability and learning pace. You can find private tutors through online platforms, language schools, or by asking for recommendations from other expats.

Online Resources: Self-Study and Language Exchange

A wealth of online resources can support your Bulgarian language learning journey. Websites, apps, and online communities offer grammar lessons, vocabulary exercises, pronunciation guides, and opportunities for language exchange with native speakers.

Popular online resources include Duolingo, Memrise, Babbel, and HelloTalk. Engaging with online communities and forums dedicated to Bulgarian language learning can connect you with other learners, provide support, and offer insights into the language and culture.

Immersion and Daily Practice: The Key to Fluency

Immersion and daily practice are crucial for mastering Bulgarian. Engage with the language in everyday life, even if it's just a few words or phrases at a time. Watch Bulgarian movies and TV shows, listen to Bulgarian music, read Bulgarian books and newspapers, and practice speaking with locals whenever possible.

Embrace opportunities to interact with native speakers, whether it's at the market, in a cafe, or with neighbors. Don't be afraid to make mistakes; language learning is a journey, and every interaction is a chance to improve.

CHAPTER FIVE: Bulgarian Banking and Finance: Managing Your Money in a New Currency '

Moving to a new country inevitably means adapting to a new financial landscape. This chapter guides you through the essentials of Bulgarian banking and finance, equipping you with the knowledge to manage your money effectively in your new home. We'll explore the currency, banking system, payment methods, and financial considerations specific to Bulgaria, helping you navigate the intricacies of your financial life as an expat.

The Bulgarian Lev (BGN): Understanding the Currency

Bulgaria's official currency is the Bulgarian lev (BGN), denoted by the symbol "лв." The lev is subdivided into 100 stotinki (ст.), although stotinki coins are rarely used in everyday transactions due to their low value.

The lev has been pegged to the euro (EUR) at a fixed exchange rate of 1.95583 leva per euro since 1999. This peg provides stability and predictability for international transactions and makes it relatively easy to calculate the approximate value of goods and services in euros.

The Bulgarian Banking System: A Stable and Accessible Network

Bulgaria's banking system is well-developed and stable, with a network of commercial banks offering a range of financial services, including current accounts, savings accounts, loans, credit cards, and money transfers. The banking sector is supervised by the Bulgarian National Bank (BNB), which ensures the stability and integrity of the financial system.

Choosing a Bank: Factors to Consider

When selecting a bank in Bulgaria, several factors come into play, including:

- **Convenience:** Choose a bank with branches or ATMs conveniently located near your home or workplace. Most banks offer online and mobile banking services, providing 24/7 access to your accounts.

- **Fees and Charges:** Compare fees and charges for various services, such as account maintenance, ATM withdrawals, and international transfers, to find a bank that offers competitive rates.

- **Customer Service:** Consider the bank's customer service reputation, including their responsiveness, helpfulness, and language support. Some banks offer English-language customer service for expats.

- **Products and Services:** Evaluate the bank's range of products and services to ensure they meet your financial needs, such as current accounts, savings accounts, loans, or investment options.

Opening a Bank Account: Steps and Requirements

Opening a bank account in Bulgaria is a straightforward process, typically requiring the following:

- **Valid Passport or ID Card:** Present your valid passport or national ID card as proof of identity.

- **Proof of Address:** Provide a document verifying your address in Bulgaria, such as a rental agreement, utility bill, or official residency registration.

- **Visa or Residence Permit:** If you're a non-EU citizen, you'll need to show your visa or residence permit as proof of legal residency in Bulgaria.

- **Initial Deposit:** Most banks require an initial deposit to open an account, which varies depending on the type of account and the bank's policy.

You can open a bank account in person at a bank branch or, in some cases, online. The bank will typically issue you a debit card and provide access to online and mobile banking services.

Payment Methods: Cash, Cards, and Transfers

Bulgaria offers a mix of payment methods, including cash, debit cards, credit cards, and bank transfers. Understanding the prevalent payment methods can help you navigate daily transactions smoothly.

Cash: Still Widely Used

Cash remains a widely accepted payment method in Bulgaria, particularly for smaller purchases and in rural areas. It's advisable to carry some cash on hand for everyday expenses, especially when traveling outside major cities.

Debit Cards: Convenient for Everyday Transactions

Debit cards are widely accepted at most shops, restaurants, and service providers in Bulgaria. They offer a convenient and secure way to pay for goods and services, eliminating the need to carry large amounts of cash.

Credit Cards: Accepted at Larger Establishments

Credit cards are generally accepted at larger establishments, such as hotels, restaurants, and supermarkets, but might not be accepted at smaller shops or in rural areas. It's advisable to check with the establishment beforehand if you plan to use a credit card.

Bank Transfers: For Larger Payments and International Transactions

Bank transfers are a common method for larger payments, such as rent or utility bills, and for international transactions. You can initiate bank transfers online, through mobile banking apps, or in person at a bank branch.

Online Payments: Gaining Popularity

Online payments are gaining popularity in Bulgaria, with many online retailers and service providers accepting payments through platforms like PayPal, Stripe, and ePay.bg. These platforms offer secure and convenient ways to make online purchases and pay for services.

Financial Considerations for Expats: Managing Your Finances

Managing your finances as an expat in Bulgaria involves adapting to a new currency, understanding local banking practices, and navigating potential financial challenges. Here are some considerations to keep in mind:

Currency Exchange: Finding the Best Rates

When exchanging currency, finding competitive exchange rates is essential to avoid unnecessary losses. Banks typically offer better exchange rates than currency exchange bureaus or airport kiosks.

It's advisable to compare exchange rates from different providers and choose the one offering the most favorable terms. Be aware of any fees or commissions associated with currency exchange transactions.

Budgeting and Cost of Living: Planning Your Expenses

Bulgaria generally has a lower cost of living than many Western European countries, but it's essential to budget your expenses carefully to ensure you can comfortably cover your needs. Consider factors like housing costs, utilities, transportation, food, entertainment, and healthcare when planning your budget.

Taxes: Understanding Your Obligations

As an expat in Bulgaria, you might be liable for taxes on your income, depending on your residency status and the source of your income. It's crucial to understand your tax obligations and seek professional advice from a tax advisor to ensure compliance with Bulgarian tax laws.

Investments: Exploring Options and Seeking Advice

If you're considering investments in Bulgaria, explore the available options, such as real estate, stocks, or bonds, and seek advice from a qualified financial advisor. Investment decisions should align with your financial goals, risk tolerance, and investment timeframe.

Retirement Planning: Securing Your Future

If you're planning for retirement in Bulgaria, consider factors like pension eligibility, healthcare costs, and lifestyle expenses. Seek guidance from a financial planner to develop a retirement plan that meets your needs and ensures a comfortable and secure future.

Remittances: Sending Money Abroad

If you need to send money abroad, compare remittance services from different providers, including banks, money transfer companies, and online platforms. Consider factors like exchange rates, fees, transfer speed, and security when choosing a remittance service.

Financial Literacy: Staying Informed and Seeking Help

Staying informed about Bulgarian financial practices, regulations, and consumer rights is essential for managing your finances effectively. The Bulgarian National Bank (BNB) and consumer protection organizations provide valuable resources and information on financial matters.

Don't hesitate to seek professional advice from a financial advisor or tax consultant if you have questions or need assistance navigating complex financial issues. They can provide personalized guidance, helping you make informed decisions and manage your finances with confidence in your new Bulgarian home.

CHAPTER SIX: Bulgarian Language Basics: Essential Phrases for Everyday Life

While English will get you by in touristy areas and some of the larger cities, learning at least the basics of the Bulgarian language is crucial for a more fulfilling and immersive experience in Bulgaria. Not only will it enable you to communicate with locals, but it also demonstrates respect for their culture and a willingness to integrate into your new community. This chapter introduces you to some essential Bulgarian phrases and expressions that will prove invaluable in everyday situations, helping you navigate your new environment with greater ease and confidence.

Greetings and Introductions: Making a Good First Impression

First impressions matter, and knowing how to greet people politely in Bulgarian sets a positive tone for your interactions. Here are some essential greetings and introductions:

Bulgarian	English
Здравейте (Zdraveйte)	Hello (formal, plural, or to a stranger)
Здравей (Zdravei)	Hello (informal, singular, to someone you know)
Добро утро (Dobro utro)	Good morning
Добър ден (Dobŭr den)	Good day / Good afternoon
Добър вечер (Dobŭr vecher)	Good evening
Довиждане (Dovizhdane)	Goodbye
Чао (Chao)	Bye (informal)
Как сте? (Kak ste?)	How are you? (formal, plural, or to a stranger)
Как си? (Kak si?)	How are you? (informal, singular, to someone you know)
Добре съм, благодаря. (Dobre sŭm, blagodarya.)	I'm fine, thank you.
Казвам се... (Kazvam se...)	My name is...

Приятно ми е. (Priyatno mi e.)   Nice to meet you.

Basic Phrases: Navigating Everyday Interactions

Equipping yourself with some basic Bulgarian phrases can make a world of difference in navigating everyday situations, from ordering food to asking for directions. Here are some essentials:

Bulgarian	English
Да (Da)	Yes
Не (Ne)	No
Моля (Molya)	Please
Благодаря (Blagodarya)	Thank you
Няма защо (Nyama za shto)	You're welcome
Извинете (Izvinete)	Excuse me
Съжалявам (Sŭzhalyavam)	Sorry
Говорите ли английски? (Govorite li angliiski?)	Do you speak English?
Не разбирам (Ne razbiram.)	I don't understand.
Можете ли да повторите? (Mozhete li da povtorite?)	Can you repeat that?
Къде е...? (Kŭde e...?)	Where is...?
Как да стигна до...? (Kak da stigna do...?)	How do I get to...?

Dining Out: Ordering Food and Drinks

Bulgarian cuisine is a delightful culinary adventure, and knowing how to order food and drinks in Bulgarian enhances the experience. Here are some phrases to help you navigate menus and communicate with restaurant staff:

Bulgarian	English
Меню, моля. (Menyu, molya.)	Menu, please.
Искам... (Iskam...)	I would like...
Какво препоръчвате? (Kakvo preporŭchvate?)	What do you recommend?
Вкусно е! (Vkusno e!)	It's delicious!

Сметката, моля. (Smetkata, molya.)   The bill, please.

Shopping: Making Purchases and Asking for Prices

Navigating shops and markets in Bulgaria becomes easier when
you know how to ask for prices, inquire about items, and make
purchases. Here are some helpful phrases:

Bulgarian	English
Колко струва това? (Kolko struva tova?)	How much does this cost?
Имате ли...? (Imate li...?)	Do you have...?
Мога ли да пробвам? (Moga li da probvam?)	Can I try this on?
Ще го взема. (Shte go vzema.)	I'll take it.

Numbers and Currency: Handling Transactions

Understanding numbers and currency is essential for handling
financial transactions in Bulgaria. Here are some key phrases:

Bulgarian	English
нула (нула)	zero
едно (edno)	one
две (dve)	two
три (tri)	three
четири (chetiri)	four
пет (pet)	five
шест (shest)	six
седем (sedem)	seven
осем (osem)	eight
девет (devet)	nine
десет (deset)	ten
лева (leva)	levs (plural of lev)
стотинки (stotinki)	stotinki (plural of stotinka)

Getting Around: Asking for Directions and Transportation

Navigating a new city or town can be challenging, especially in a foreign language. Here are some phrases to help you ask for directions and find your way around:

Bulgarian	English
Къде е...? (Kŭde e...?)	Where is...?
Как да стигна до...? (Kak da stigna do...?)	How do I get to...?
автобус (avtobus)	bus
влак (vlak)	train
такси (taksi)	taxi

Time and Dates: Scheduling Appointments and Events

Knowing how to express time and dates is crucial for scheduling appointments, making plans, and understanding event schedules. Here are some key phrases:

Bulgarian	English
Колко е часът? (Kolko e chasŭt?)	What time is it?
час (chas)	hour
минути (minuti)	minutes
ден (den)	day
седмица (sedmitsa)	week
месец (mesets)	month
година (godina)	year

Pronunciation Tips: Mastering the Sounds of Bulgarian

Bulgarian pronunciation can seem challenging at first, but understanding a few key rules can make a significant difference.

- **Stress:** Bulgarian words are typically stressed on the first syllable.

- **Vowels:** Bulgarian has six vowel sounds, pronounced similarly to their English counterparts, with a few exceptions. For example, the letter "ъ" (pronounced "ŭ") represents a short, neutral vowel sound, similar to the "a" in "sofa."

- **Consonants:** Most Bulgarian consonants are pronounced similarly to their English counterparts, but some require special attention. For example, the letter "ч" (pronounced "ch") represents a soft "ch" sound, as in "cheese," while "ш" (pronounced "sh") represents a "sh" sound, as in "ship."

Language Learning Resources: Expanding Your Bulgarian Skills

Numerous resources can help you expand your Bulgarian language skills beyond the basics. Consider the following:

- **Language Schools:** Enroll in a structured Bulgarian language course at a language school to learn grammar, vocabulary, and conversational skills.

- **Private Tutors:** Hire a private tutor for personalized instruction and flexible scheduling.

- **Online Resources:** Utilize online language learning platforms like Duolingo, Memrise, and Babbel for self-study and interactive exercises.

- **Language Exchange Partners:** Find language exchange partners online or through local language groups to practice speaking and improve your conversational fluency.

- **Bulgarian Media:** Watch Bulgarian movies and TV shows, listen to Bulgarian music, and read Bulgarian books and newspapers to immerse yourself in the language and culture.

Embrace the Journey: Learning a Language Takes Time and Practice

Learning a new language is a rewarding journey, but it takes time, patience, and consistent practice. Embrace the process, don't be afraid to make mistakes, and celebrate your progress along the way. The effort you invest in learning Bulgarian will pay dividends in your ability to connect with locals, navigate your new environment, and enrich your expat experience in Bulgaria.

CHAPTER SEVEN: Transportation in Bulgaria: From Public Transport to Car Ownership

Getting around in a new country is essential for both practical daily life and exploring your new surroundings. This chapter delves into the various transportation options available in Bulgaria, from navigating the public transport system to understanding the intricacies of car ownership. We'll provide you with insights and practical tips to help you traverse the Bulgarian landscape with ease and confidence, whether you're commuting to work, exploring historical sites, or venturing into the scenic countryside.

Public Transportation: A Network of Buses, Trains, and Trams

Bulgaria boasts a comprehensive public transportation system, encompassing buses, trains, trams, and trolleybuses, connecting cities, towns, and villages across the country. Public transport is generally affordable, reliable, and a convenient way to get around, especially in urban areas.

Urban Transport: Navigating Cities and Towns

Within cities and towns, buses, trams, and trolleybuses are the primary modes of public transport. These systems are typically well-maintained, frequent, and cover most areas of the urban landscape.

- **Buses:** Buses are the most common form of public transport in Bulgaria, with extensive networks operating within cities and connecting them to surrounding towns and villages. Bus stops are usually marked with signs indicating the routes served and approximate arrival times. You can purchase tickets from the driver or at designated kiosks, and it's customary to validate your ticket upon boarding.

- **Trams:** Trams operate in several larger cities, including Sofia, Plovdiv, and Varna, providing a convenient and efficient way to travel along designated routes. Tram stops are marked with signs indicating the routes and schedules. Tickets can be purchased from vending machines at tram stops or from conductors on board.

- **Trolleybuses:** Trolleybuses, electric buses powered by overhead wires, operate in some cities, offering a quieter and more environmentally friendly alternative to traditional buses. They follow designated routes, with stops marked with signs indicating schedules. Tickets can be purchased from the driver or at designated kiosks.

Intercity Transport: Connecting Cities and Regions

For traveling between cities and regions, trains and long-distance buses provide reliable and comfortable options.

- **Trains:** Bulgaria's railway network connects major cities and towns across the country. Trains are generally comfortable, with various classes of service offering different levels of amenities. You can purchase tickets at train stations, online, or through travel agents. It's advisable to book tickets in advance, especially for popular routes or during peak travel seasons.

- **Long-Distance Buses:** Numerous private bus companies operate long-distance routes, connecting cities and towns throughout Bulgaria. Buses vary in comfort and amenities, with some offering reclining seats, air conditioning, and onboard Wi-Fi. You can purchase tickets at bus stations, online, or through travel agents.

Public Transport Tips: Navigating the System

Here are some practical tips for navigating the Bulgarian public transportation system:

- **Plan Your Route:** Use online journey planners or mobile apps to map your route, check schedules, and estimate travel times. Popular apps include Google Maps, Moovit, and the Bulgarian State Railways app.

- **Purchase Tickets in Advance:** Buy tickets in advance for trains and long-distance buses, especially during peak travel seasons, to secure your seat and avoid queues.

- **Validate Your Ticket:** Always validate your ticket upon boarding buses, trams, or trolleybuses to avoid fines. Ticket validation machines are usually located near the entrance doors.

- **Be Mindful of Peak Hours:** Public transport can be crowded during peak commuting hours in urban areas. Allow extra travel time if you're traveling during these periods.

- **Learn Basic Phrases:** Knowing a few basic Bulgarian phrases, such as "Where is the bus stop?" or "What time does the train leave?" can be helpful when seeking information or assistance.

Taxis: Convenient but Exercise Caution

Taxis are readily available in Bulgaria, offering a convenient way to get around, especially for short distances or when traveling with luggage. However, it's essential to exercise caution when using taxis, as scams and overcharging can occur.

Licensed Taxis: Identifying Legitimate Services

Licensed taxis are typically yellow, with a taxi sign on the roof and a meter inside. They are required to display their license number and driver's ID card on the dashboard.

Ordering Taxis: Hailing, Phone Dispatch, or Apps

You can hail taxis on the street, order them by phone through dispatch services, or use taxi-hailing apps like Maxim, TaxiMe, and Yellow Taxi. Apps often provide estimated fares and allow you to track the taxi's location.

Taxi Tips: Avoiding Scams and Overcharging

Here are some tips to avoid scams and overcharging when using taxis in Bulgaria:

- **Use Licensed Taxis:** Only use licensed taxis that display their license number and driver's ID card.

- **Agree on the Fare Beforehand:** If you're hailing a taxi on the street, agree on the fare before getting in to avoid disputes later.

- **Ensure the Meter is Running:** Check that the meter is running from the start of the journey. If it's not, ask the driver to turn it on.

- **Be Aware of Common Scams:** Be wary of drivers who take unnecessarily long routes, refuse to use the meter, or claim the meter is broken.

- **Report Any Issues:** If you encounter any problems or suspect overcharging, report the incident to the local authorities or your embassy.

Car Ownership: A Mixed Bag of Convenience and Challenges

Owning a car in Bulgaria offers convenience and flexibility, especially for exploring the countryside or venturing off the beaten path. However, car ownership also comes with its share of challenges, including traffic congestion in urban areas, road conditions, and parking availability.

Buying a Car: New or Used Options

You can purchase cars in Bulgaria from authorized dealerships, used car lots, or through private sellers. New cars come with warranties and financing options, while used cars offer more affordable prices but might require inspections and repairs.

Registering a Car: Navigating the Bureaucracy

To register a car in Bulgaria, you'll need to provide the following documents:

- **Valid Passport or ID Card:** Your valid passport or national ID card as proof of identity.

- **Proof of Address:** A document verifying your address in Bulgaria, such as a rental agreement, utility bill, or official residency registration.

- **Vehicle Registration Certificate:** The original vehicle registration certificate, known as "голям талон" (golyam talon), issued by the previous owner.

- **Technical Inspection Certificate:** A valid technical inspection certificate, confirming the car's roadworthiness.

- **Insurance Policy:** Proof of valid car insurance, including third-party liability coverage, which is mandatory in Bulgaria.

You can register your car at the local traffic police department, known as "KAT" (KAT). The registration process involves paying fees and receiving new license plates.

Driving in Bulgaria: Rules and Regulations

Driving in Bulgaria requires adherence to local traffic rules and regulations. Here are some key points to remember:

- **Drive on the Right:** Traffic in Bulgaria drives on the right side of the road.

- **Seat Belts Mandatory:** Wearing seat belts is mandatory for all passengers in the vehicle.

- **Speed Limits:** Speed limits vary depending on the type of road and the area. Generally, the speed limit in built-up areas is 50 km/h (31 mph), on open roads 90 km/h (56 mph), and on highways 140 km/h (87 mph).

- **Blood Alcohol Limit:** The legal blood alcohol limit for drivers is 0.05%. Driving under the influence of alcohol is strictly prohibited and carries severe penalties.

- **Headlights Required:** Headlights must be turned on at all times, even during daylight hours.

- **Winter Tires:** Winter tires are mandatory from November 1st to March 31st, or when road conditions require them.

- **Vignette Required for Highways:** To drive on Bulgarian highways, you need to purchase a vignette, a road toll sticker, available at gas stations, post offices, and border crossings.

Parking: Availability and Regulations

Parking availability can be a challenge in urban areas, especially in city centers. Street parking is often limited and regulated by parking zones, requiring payment at designated parking meters or through mobile apps. Off-street parking garages and lots provide alternatives, but fees can vary depending on location and duration.

Car Maintenance and Repairs: Finding Reliable Services

Bulgaria has a network of car repair shops and service centers, offering a range of maintenance and repair services. You can find authorized dealerships for specific car brands, as well as independent garages specializing in various types of vehicles.

Car Ownership Tips: Navigating the Challenges

Here are some tips for navigating the challenges of car ownership in Bulgaria:

- **Research Car Prices and Availability:** Compare prices and availability from different sources, including dealerships, used car lots, and private sellers, to find the best deal.

- **Get a Pre-Purchase Inspection:** If you're buying a used car, get a pre-purchase inspection from a qualified mechanic to assess its condition and potential repair costs.

- **Understand the Registration Process:** Familiarize yourself with the car registration process and gather all the necessary documents to avoid delays.

- **Learn Basic Bulgarian Road Signs:** Understanding basic Bulgarian road signs is essential for safe driving.

- **Be Mindful of Traffic Conditions:** Traffic congestion can be heavy in urban areas, especially during peak commuting hours. Allow extra travel time and plan alternative routes if necessary.

- **Find Reliable Parking Options:** Research parking options in advance, especially if you're driving in city centers or areas with limited parking availability.

- **Secure Car Insurance:** Ensure you have valid car insurance, including third-party liability coverage, which is mandatory in Bulgaria.

Other Transportation Options: Exploring Alternatives

Beyond public transport and car ownership, Bulgaria offers other transportation options, each with its advantages and considerations.

Cycling: A Healthy and Eco-Friendly Choice

Cycling is a popular mode of transportation in Bulgaria, especially in cities with dedicated bike lanes and paths. It's a healthy, eco-friendly, and often efficient way to get around, particularly for shorter distances.

Ride-Sharing: Convenient and Cost-Effective

Ride-sharing services like Uber and Bolt operate in major Bulgarian cities, offering a convenient and often cost-effective alternative to taxis. You can order rides through their mobile apps, track the driver's location, and pay for your trip through the app.

Car Rentals: Flexibility for Exploring the Country

Car rental companies operate in Bulgaria, providing short-term and long-term car rentals. Renting a car can be a convenient option for exploring the countryside, visiting remote areas, or traveling with a group.

Domestic Flights: Connecting Major Cities

Bulgaria has several domestic airports, connecting major cities like Sofia, Varna, and Burgas. Domestic flights can be a time-saving option for long-distance travel within the country.

Transportation Tips for Expats: Making Informed Choices

Navigating the transportation landscape in Bulgaria requires understanding the available options, their advantages, and potential challenges. Here are some tips to help you make informed transportation choices as an expat:

- **Consider Your Needs and Lifestyle:** Evaluate your transportation needs based on your lifestyle, daily commute, and exploration plans.

- **Research Different Options:** Explore the various transportation options available in your area, comparing their costs, convenience, and reliability.

- **Plan Your Routes and Schedules:** Use online journey planners or mobile apps to plan your routes, check schedules, and estimate travel times.

- **Learn Basic Bulgarian Phrases:** Knowing a few basic Bulgarian phrases related to transportation can be helpful when seeking information or assistance.

- **Embrace Flexibility:** Be prepared to adapt your transportation choices based on traffic conditions, weather, and availability.

Whether you're relying on public transport, owning a car, or exploring alternative options, understanding the intricacies of transportation in Bulgaria will empower you to navigate your new environment with ease and confidence, opening up a world of possibilities for both practical daily life and adventurous exploration.

CHAPTER EIGHT: Bulgarian Cuisine: A Culinary Journey Through Traditional Dishes

Bulgarian cuisine is a delightful fusion of Balkan, Mediterranean, and Middle Eastern influences, resulting in a rich tapestry of flavors and textures. Fresh, seasonal ingredients are at the heart of Bulgarian cooking, with an emphasis on grilled meats, hearty stews, colorful salads, and savory pastries. This chapter takes you on a culinary journey through some of Bulgaria's most beloved traditional dishes, providing you with insights into the unique flavors and culinary traditions that await you in your new home.

Shopska Salad: A Refreshing Bulgarian Classic

No culinary exploration of Bulgaria is complete without savoring the iconic Shopska salad, a refreshing and colorful staple found on almost every restaurant menu. This simple yet satisfying salad embodies the essence of Bulgarian cuisine, showcasing fresh, seasonal ingredients and a harmonious balance of flavors.

Ingredient	Quantity
Tomatoes	4, diced
Cucumbers	2, diced
Red Onion	1, finely chopped
Roasted Red Peppers	2, sliced
Bulgarian Feta Cheese (Sirene)	200g, crumbled
Parsley	A handful, chopped
Olive Oil	To taste
Salt	To taste
Black Pepper	To taste

Preparation:

1. Combine the diced tomatoes, cucumbers, and chopped red onion in a large bowl.

2. Add the sliced roasted red peppers and crumbled feta cheese.

3. Sprinkle with chopped parsley.

4. Drizzle with olive oil and season with salt and black pepper to taste.

5. Gently toss the ingredients to combine.

6. Serve chilled.

Variations:

- Some variations of Shopska salad include green peppers, olives, or vinegar.

- You can also add a sprinkle of dried oregano or summer savory for an extra layer of flavor.

Tarator: A Cooling Summer Soup

Tarator is a cold soup traditionally enjoyed during the hot summer months. This refreshing and tangy soup is made with yogurt, cucumbers, dill, walnuts, and garlic, offering a welcome respite from the heat.

Ingredient	Quantity
Yogurt	500g, plain
Cucumbers	2, peeled and finely chopped
Dill	A handful, chopped
Walnuts	50g, chopped
Garlic	2 cloves, minced
Water	1/2 cup
Olive Oil	To taste
Salt	To taste

Preparation:

1. In a large bowl, whisk together the yogurt, chopped cucumbers, dill, walnuts, and minced garlic.

2. Gradually add the water, whisking continuously until the soup reaches your desired consistency.

3. Drizzle with olive oil and season with salt to taste.

4. Refrigerate for at least an hour before serving to allow the flavors to meld.

Variations:

- Some variations of Tarator include adding a tablespoon of sunflower oil or a squeeze of lemon juice.

- You can also add a pinch of ground cumin or paprika for a subtle spice note.

Banitsa: A Savory Pastry for Every Occasion

Banitsa is a beloved Bulgarian pastry made with layers of thin phyllo dough, filled with a variety of savory or sweet ingredients. It's a versatile dish enjoyed for breakfast, brunch, or as a snack, and its flaky, golden crust and flavorful fillings make it a true culinary delight.

Traditional Savory Filling:

Ingredient	Quantity
Bulgarian Feta Cheese (Sirene)	400g, crumbled
Eggs	4, beaten
Yogurt	1/2 cup, plain
Baking Soda	1/2 teaspoon
Butter	100g, melted

Preparation:

1. Preheat oven to 180°C (350°F).

2. In a large bowl, combine the crumbled feta cheese, beaten eggs, yogurt, and baking soda.

3. Lay out one sheet of phyllo dough on a lightly greased baking sheet.

4. Brush the phyllo dough with melted butter.

5. Spread a thin layer of the cheese filling over the buttered phyllo dough.

6. Repeat layers 3-5, using all the phyllo dough and cheese filling.

7. Tuck the edges of the phyllo dough to enclose the filling.

8. Brush the top layer of phyllo dough with melted butter.

9. Bake for 30-40 minutes, or until golden brown and flaky.

Variations:

- Banitsa can be filled with a variety of other savory ingredients, such as spinach, leeks, mushrooms, or ground meat.

- You can also add a sprinkle of dried dill, parsley, or savory spices like paprika or black pepper to the cheese filling.

Kavarma: A Hearty Meat Stew

Kavarma is a hearty and flavorful meat stew, a staple of Bulgarian cuisine, often served in clay pots to retain its warmth and enhance its rustic charm. This dish typically features pork, chicken, or veal, simmered with onions, peppers, tomatoes, and a blend of aromatic spices.

Ingredient	Quantity
Pork, Chicken, or Veal	1kg, cubed
Onions	2, chopped

Green Peppers	2, chopped
Red Peppers	1, chopped
Tomatoes	4, chopped
Garlic	4 cloves, minced
Red Wine	1/2 cup
Paprika	1 tablespoon
Black Pepper	1 teaspoon
Bay Leaves	2
Olive Oil	To taste
Salt	To taste

Preparation:

1. Heat olive oil in a large pot or Dutch oven over medium heat.

2. Add the cubed meat and cook until browned on all sides.

3. Add the chopped onions, green peppers, red peppers, and minced garlic.

4. Cook until the vegetables are softened, about 5-7 minutes.

5. Stir in the chopped tomatoes, red wine, paprika, black pepper, bay leaves, and salt.

6. Bring to a simmer, cover, and cook for 1-2 hours, or until the meat is tender.

Variations:

- Some variations of Kavarma include adding mushrooms, carrots, or potatoes.

- You can also adjust the spiciness by adding more or less paprika or black pepper.

Kyufteta: Grilled Meatballs

Kyufteta are flavorful grilled meatballs, a popular street food and a staple at Bulgarian barbecues. These juicy and savory meatballs are typically made with a mix of ground pork and beef, seasoned with onions, garlic, and spices, and grilled to perfection.

Ingredient	Quantity
Ground Pork	500g
Ground Beef	500g
Onions	1, finely chopped
Garlic	3 cloves, minced
Breadcrumbs	1/2 cup
Milk	1/4 cup
Eggs	1, beaten
Paprika	1 teaspoon
Cumin	1/2 teaspoon
Black Pepper	1/2 teaspoon
Salt	To taste

Preparation:

1. In a large bowl, combine the ground pork, ground beef, chopped onion, minced garlic, breadcrumbs, milk, beaten egg, paprika, cumin, black pepper, and salt.

2. Mix well with your hands until all the ingredients are evenly incorporated.

3. Shape the mixture into small, round meatballs.

4. Preheat a grill or grill pan over medium heat.

5. Grill the meatballs for 10-15 minutes, turning occasionally, until cooked through.

Variations:

- Some variations of Kyufteta include adding chopped parsley or dill to the meat mixture.

- You can also serve the meatballs with a side of yogurt sauce, tomato sauce, or a simple salad.

Sarmi: Stuffed Cabbage Rolls

Sarmi are stuffed cabbage rolls, a traditional Bulgarian dish often enjoyed during the colder months. These hearty and flavorful rolls feature cabbage leaves filled with a mixture of rice, ground meat, onions, and spices, simmered in a tomato-based sauce.

Ingredient	Quantity
Cabbage	1 head
Ground Pork or Beef	500g
Rice	1/2 cup, uncooked
Onions	1, chopped
Carrots	1, grated
Tomatoes	4, chopped
Tomato Paste	2 tablespoons
Paprika	1 tablespoon
Black Pepper	1/2 teaspoon
Bay Leaves	2
Olive Oil	To taste
Salt	To taste

Preparation:

1. Remove the core from the cabbage head.

2. Blanch the cabbage leaves in boiling water for a few minutes until softened.

3. In a large bowl, combine the ground meat, uncooked rice, chopped onion, grated carrot, paprika, black pepper, and salt.

4. Place a spoonful of the meat mixture onto each cabbage leaf.

5. Roll up the cabbage leaves to enclose the filling, tucking in the sides.

6. Heat olive oil in a large pot or Dutch oven over medium heat.

7. Add the chopped tomatoes and tomato paste.

8. Cook for a few minutes, stirring occasionally.

9. Arrange the stuffed cabbage rolls in the pot, seam side down.

10. Add water to cover the rolls.

11. Add the bay leaves and salt.

12. Bring to a simmer, cover, and cook for 1-2 hours, or until the rice and meat are cooked through.

Variations:

- Some variations of Sarmi include adding chopped parsley or dill to the meat mixture.

- You can also use sauerkraut leaves instead of fresh cabbage leaves for a tangier flavor.

Musaka: A Layered Potato and Meat Casserole

Musaka is a beloved Bulgarian dish, a comforting and flavorful casserole featuring layers of potatoes, ground meat, and a creamy béchamel sauce. This dish is baked to perfection, creating a harmonious blend of textures and flavors that is sure to satisfy.

Ingredient	Quantity
Potatoes	1kg, peeled and sliced
Ground Pork or Beef	500g
Onions	1, chopped

Tomatoes	4, chopped
Tomato Paste	2 tablespoons
Paprika	1 tablespoon
Black Pepper	1/2 teaspoon
Olive Oil	To taste
Salt	To taste
Béchamel Sauce:	
Butter	50g
Flour	50g
Milk	500ml
Eggs	2, beaten
Nutmeg	A pinch

Preparation:

1. Preheat oven to 180°C (350°F).

2. Heat olive oil in a large pan over medium heat.

3. Add the ground meat and cook until browned.

4. Add the chopped onion and cook until softened.

5. Stir in the chopped tomatoes, tomato paste, paprika, black pepper, and salt.

6. Cook for a few minutes, stirring occasionally.

7. Arrange a layer of sliced potatoes in a greased baking dish.

8. Top with the meat mixture.

9. Repeat layers 7-8, ending with a layer of potatoes.

10. To make the béchamel sauce, melt the butter in a saucepan over medium heat.

11. Whisk in the flour and cook for a minute.

12. Gradually whisk in the milk until smooth.

13. Cook until the sauce thickens, stirring constantly.

14. Remove from heat and stir in the beaten eggs and nutmeg.

15. Pour the béchamel sauce over the potatoes.

16. Bake for 45-60 minutes, or until golden brown and bubbly.

Variations:

- Some variations of Musaka include adding grated cheese to the béchamel sauce or sprinkling it on top of the potatoes before baking.

- You can also add other vegetables, such as eggplant or zucchini, to the meat mixture.

Bulgarian Yogurt: A Culinary Staple

Bulgarian yogurt, known as кисело мляко (kiselo mlyako), is renowned for its unique flavor, creamy texture, and health benefits. This yogurt is made with a specific strain of bacteria, Lactobacillus bulgaricus, which gives it its distinctive tangy taste and thick consistency.

Bulgarian yogurt is a versatile ingredient used in various dishes, from salads and soups to sauces and desserts. It's also enjoyed on its own, often served with honey, fruit, or nuts.

Bulgarian Cheeses: A Variety of Flavors and Textures

Bulgaria boasts a rich tradition of cheesemaking, with a wide variety of cheeses to tantalize your taste buds. Here are a few notable Bulgarian cheeses:

- **Bulgarian Feta Cheese (Sirene):** A brined white cheese made from sheep's milk, cow's milk, or a blend of both. It has a salty, tangy flavor and a crumbly texture. Sirene is a staple ingredient in many Bulgarian dishes, including Shopska salad and Banitsa.

- **Kashkaval:** A yellow, semi-hard cheese made from sheep's milk, cow's milk, or a blend of both. It has a mild, nutty flavor and a slightly elastic texture. Kashkaval is often used in grilled cheese sandwiches, salads, and pastries.

- **Yellow Cheese:** A generic term for a variety of yellow cheeses, often similar in flavor and texture to cheddar. Yellow cheese is commonly used in sandwiches, pizzas, and other dishes.

Bulgarian Wine: A Rich History and Diverse Varietals

Bulgaria has a long and storied history of winemaking, dating back to Thracian times. The country's diverse climate and terroir produce a wide range of wine styles, from crisp whites and fruity rosés to full-bodied reds.

Some notable Bulgarian grape varietals include:

- **Mavrud:** A red grape variety indigenous to Bulgaria, known for producing full-bodied, robust wines with notes of dark fruit, spice, and tobacco.

- **Rubin:** A red grape variety created in Bulgaria, producing wines with a ruby-red color and aromas of red berries, cherries, and spices.

- **Dimyat:** A white grape variety indigenous to Bulgaria, known for producing aromatic, dry white wines with notes of citrus, melon, and herbs.

Rakia: A Traditional Fruit Brandy

Rakia is a traditional fruit brandy widely enjoyed in Bulgaria and other Balkan countries. It's typically made from grapes, plums, apricots, or other fruits, fermented and distilled to produce a potent and flavorful spirit.

Rakia is often served chilled as an aperitif or digestif, and it's also used in cocktails and traditional Bulgarian desserts.

Bulgarian Desserts: Sweet Treats and Indulgences

Bulgarian cuisine offers a tempting array of sweet treats and indulgences. Here are a few notable Bulgarian desserts:

- **Baklava:** A sweet pastry made with layers of thin phyllo dough, filled with chopped nuts and sweetened with syrup or honey.

- **Garash Cake:** A rich chocolate cake with layers of walnuts and chocolate icing.

- **Tikvenik:** A sweet pumpkin pastry made with phyllo dough, filled with grated pumpkin, sugar, and spices.

Exploring Bulgarian Cuisine: A Culinary Adventure

Embracing Bulgarian cuisine is an integral part of the expat experience, offering a delightful culinary adventure and a deeper connection to the local culture. Here are some tips for exploring Bulgarian culinary delights:

- **Dine at Traditional Bulgarian Restaurants (Механа - mehana):** These restaurants offer authentic Bulgarian dishes, often served in a rustic and welcoming atmosphere.

- **Visit Local Markets (пазар - pazar):** Explore the abundance of fresh, seasonal produce, cheeses, and meats at local markets to get a taste of the local ingredients that form the foundation of Bulgarian cuisine.

- **Attend Culinary Festivals and Events:** Many towns and cities host culinary festivals and events throughout the year, showcasing regional specialties and traditional cooking techniques.

- **Learn Basic Bulgarian Food-Related Phrases:** Knowing a few basic phrases, such as "I would like to try this," or "It's delicious," can enhance your dining experiences and interactions with restaurant staff.

- **Be Adventurous and Open to New Flavors:** Step outside your comfort zone and try dishes you might not be familiar with. You might be surprised by the culinary gems you discover.

- **Embrace the Slow Food Culture:** Bulgarian meals are often leisurely affairs, meant to be savored and enjoyed in good company. Take your time, enjoy the food, and embrace the relaxed dining experience.

Bulgarian cuisine is a testament to the country's rich history, diverse influences, and passion for fresh, flavorful ingredients. As you embark on your culinary journey, you'll discover a world of culinary delights that will tantalize your taste buds and provide a deeper appreciation for the heart and soul of Bulgarian culture.

CHAPTER NINE: Shopping and Groceries: Finding Your Way Around Bulgarian Markets

Navigating the shopping landscape in a new country can be an adventure in itself, offering glimpses into local customs, products, and the rhythm of daily life. This chapter explores the diverse shopping and grocery options available in Bulgaria, from bustling open-air markets to modern supermarkets and shopping malls. We'll guide you through the nuances of finding fresh produce, household essentials, and unique Bulgarian products, helping you navigate the shopping scene with confidence and discover the treasures that await.

Open-Air Markets (пазар - pazar): A Sensory Feast of Freshness

Open-air markets, known as "пазар" (pazar), are a vibrant and integral part of Bulgarian culture, offering a sensory feast of fresh produce, local delicacies, and a glimpse into the heart of community life. These bustling markets are a treasure trove of seasonal fruits and vegetables, aromatic herbs and spices, locally produced cheeses and meats, and an array of household goods, clothing, and souvenirs.

Seasonal Bounty: A Rainbow of Flavors

Bulgarian markets are a testament to the country's agricultural heritage, bursting with a rainbow of colors and flavors as the seasons change. From juicy tomatoes and crisp cucumbers in summer to plump grapes and sweet figs in autumn, each season brings its own bounty of fresh produce.

Vendors proudly display their wares, often grown in their own gardens or sourced from nearby farms, ensuring quality and freshness. Engage with the vendors, ask about their products, and don't hesitate to sample the fruits and vegetables before you buy.

Local Delicacies: Cheeses, Meats, and More

Bulgarian markets are also a haven for local delicacies, showcasing the country's rich culinary traditions. Stalls overflowing with various cheeses, from creamy sirene to tangy kashkaval, invite you to sample the flavors of Bulgarian cheesemaking.

Meat vendors offer a selection of fresh cuts, cured meats, and sausages, often prepared using traditional methods passed down through generations. Engage with the vendors, inquire about the different types of meats and sausages, and discover new flavors to tantalize your taste buds.

Beyond Food: A Tapestry of Goods

Bulgarian markets extend beyond food, offering a tapestry of goods and services. Stalls selling household items, clothing, shoes, toys, and souvenirs add to the vibrant atmosphere. You can find everything from kitchenware and cleaning supplies to traditional Bulgarian crafts and handcrafted jewelry.

Bargaining: A Gentle Art

Bargaining is a common practice in Bulgarian markets, especially for non-food items. It's a gentle art that involves respectful negotiation and a bit of good-natured banter. Don't be afraid to engage in friendly haggling, but always be respectful and avoid being overly aggressive.

Market Tips: Navigating the Pazar Experience

Here are some tips for navigating the Bulgarian market experience:

- **Arrive Early:** Markets are busiest in the mornings, as locals stock up on fresh produce and daily essentials. Arriving early ensures a wider selection and a less crowded atmosphere.

- **Bring Cash:** Most vendors at Bulgarian markets prefer cash payments. It's advisable to carry smaller denominations for easier transactions.

- **Engage with Vendors:** Don't hesitate to ask questions, sample products, and engage in friendly conversation with the vendors. It's a great way to learn about local products, culinary traditions, and the rhythm of market life.

- **Respect the Culture:** Be mindful of local customs and etiquette. Avoid touching produce without asking, be respectful when bargaining, and dress appropriately.

- **Enjoy the Sensory Experience:** Bulgarian markets are a feast for the senses, with vibrant colors, enticing aromas, and lively sounds. Take your time, soak in the atmosphere, and enjoy the unique cultural experience.

Supermarkets: Modern Convenience and a Wider Selection

Supermarkets have become increasingly prevalent in Bulgaria, offering a modern and convenient shopping experience with a wider selection of products, including imported goods, packaged foods, and household essentials. Major supermarket chains like Billa, Kaufland, Lidl, and Fantastico operate throughout the country, providing a familiar shopping environment for expats.

Product Range: From Local to International

Bulgarian supermarkets offer a diverse range of products, catering to both local tastes and expat preferences. You can find fresh produce, dairy products, meats, baked goods, canned goods, frozen foods, snacks, beverages, and household essentials.

Many supermarkets also stock imported goods, catering to the growing expat community and offering a taste of home for those seeking familiar brands and products.

Pricing and Promotions: Finding Value

Supermarket prices are generally competitive, with regular promotions and discounts on various products. Loyalty programs and store cards offer additional savings and benefits. It's advisable to compare prices between different supermarkets and take advantage of promotions to maximize your budget.

Payment Methods: Cash, Cards, and Self-Checkout

Bulgarian supermarkets typically accept cash, debit cards, and credit cards. Some supermarkets also offer self-checkout kiosks, providing a faster and more efficient checkout experience.

Supermarket Tips: Navigating the Aisles

Here are some tips for navigating Bulgarian supermarkets:

- **Bring Your Own Bags:** Most supermarkets charge for plastic bags, so it's advisable to bring your own reusable bags.

- **Check the Expiration Dates:** Always check the expiration dates on products, especially for fresh produce, dairy, and meats.

- **Utilize Loyalty Programs:** Sign up for loyalty programs or store cards to earn points, discounts, and other benefits.

- **Explore the Local Products:** Venture beyond familiar brands and explore the local Bulgarian products on offer.

You might discover new favorites and hidden culinary gems.

Shopping Malls: A Blend of Retail Therapy and Entertainment

Shopping malls have emerged as popular destinations in Bulgaria, offering a blend of retail therapy, entertainment, and dining options. These modern complexes house a variety of stores, from international fashion brands to local boutiques, as well as cinemas, restaurants, cafes, and entertainment centers.

International and Local Brands: A Diverse Retail Landscape

Bulgarian shopping malls showcase a diverse retail landscape, with a mix of international and local brands. You can find everything from clothing, shoes, and accessories to electronics, home goods, and cosmetics.

Local boutiques offer unique Bulgarian products, such as handcrafted jewelry, traditional crafts, and designer clothing. Exploring these boutiques provides a glimpse into the country's creative talent and offers opportunities to support local businesses.

Entertainment and Dining: A One-Stop Destination

Shopping malls often serve as one-stop destinations, offering entertainment options like cinemas, bowling alleys, and amusement centers. Dining choices range from fast food chains to casual restaurants and cafes, catering to various tastes and budgets.

Shopping Mall Tips: Navigating the Experience

Here are some tips for navigating Bulgarian shopping malls:

- **Check Opening Hours:** Shopping malls typically have longer opening hours than individual stores, often extending into the evenings and weekends.

- **Utilize Mall Maps and Directories:** Most malls provide maps and directories to help you navigate the complex and locate specific stores.

- **Take Advantage of Promotions:** Many stores offer promotions, discounts, and sales, especially during holidays and special events.

- **Explore the Dining Options:** Take a break from shopping and explore the mall's dining options, ranging from quick bites to leisurely meals.

Specialized Stores: Finding Niche Products and Services

Beyond markets, supermarkets, and shopping malls, Bulgaria has a network of specialized stores catering to specific needs and interests. These stores offer a wider selection and expert knowledge in their respective fields.

Electronics and Appliances: Staying Connected and Equipped

Electronics stores like Technopolis, Technomarket, and Zora offer a wide range of electronics, appliances, and gadgets, from smartphones and laptops to TVs, refrigerators, and washing machines. These stores often provide warranties, financing options, and technical support.

Home Goods and Furniture: Furnishing Your Bulgarian Home

Home goods and furniture stores like IKEA, JYSK, and Aiko offer a variety of furniture, home decor, kitchenware, bedding, and other household essentials. These stores cater to various tastes and budgets, with options ranging from modern and minimalist to traditional and rustic.

Clothing and Fashion: Expressing Your Style

Clothing and fashion stores abound in Bulgaria, offering a diverse range of styles, brands, and price points. International fashion brands like Zara, H&M, and Mango have a presence in major cities, while local boutiques showcase Bulgarian designers and independent labels.

Books and Stationery: Fueling Your Literary Pursuits

Bookstores like Хеликон (Helikon) and Orange Center offer a wide selection of books in Bulgarian and English, as well as stationery, office supplies, and gifts. These stores often host book signings, author events, and other literary gatherings.

Pharmacies: Accessing Medications and Healthcare Essentials

Pharmacies (аптека - apteka) are readily available in Bulgaria, offering a range of prescription and over-the-counter medications, as well as healthcare essentials like vitamins, supplements, and personal care products.

Specialized Store Tips: Finding What You Need

Here are some tips for navigating specialized stores in Bulgaria:

- **Research Online:** Check online directories, store websites, and customer reviews to identify stores that specialize in the products or services you're seeking.

- **Ask for Recommendations:** Inquire with locals, expats, and colleagues for recommendations on reputable stores and service providers.

- **Compare Prices:** Don't hesitate to compare prices between different stores to ensure you're getting a fair deal.

- **Inquire about Warranties and Returns:** Check the store's policies on warranties, returns, and exchanges before making a purchase.

- **Seek Expert Advice:** Don't hesitate to ask store staff for advice, recommendations, or product demonstrations.

Online Shopping: A Growing Trend in Bulgaria

Online shopping is gaining popularity in Bulgaria, offering a convenient and increasingly accessible alternative to traditional brick-and-mortar stores. Major online retailers like eMag.bg, Ozone.bg, and Fashion Days offer a wide range of products, from electronics and appliances to clothing, home goods, and books.

Advantages of Online Shopping: Convenience, Selection, and Comparison

Online shopping offers several advantages, including:

- **Convenience:** Shop from the comfort of your home, anytime, anywhere.

- **Wider Selection:** Access a broader range of products, often including items not available in local stores.

- **Price Comparison:** Easily compare prices from different retailers to find the best deals.

- **Product Reviews:** Read customer reviews and ratings to get insights into product quality and performance.

- **Home Delivery:** Have your purchases delivered directly to your doorstep.

Online Shopping Tips: Navigating the Virtual Marketplace

Here are some tips for navigating the online shopping landscape in Bulgaria:

- **Choose Reputable Retailers:** Shop from well-established and trustworthy online retailers with a good reputation for customer service and secure payment processing.

- **Read Product Descriptions Carefully:** Pay close attention to product descriptions, specifications, and customer reviews before making a purchase.

- **Check Shipping Costs and Delivery Times:** Factor in shipping costs and delivery times when comparing prices and making purchase decisions.

- **Understand Return Policies:** Familiarize yourself with the retailer's return policies in case you need to return or exchange a product.

- **Secure Payment Methods:** Use secure payment methods, such as credit cards or PayPal, to protect your financial information.

Shopping and Grocery Tips for Expats: Embracing the Bulgarian Experience

Navigating the shopping and grocery scene in Bulgaria offers a unique opportunity to immerse yourself in the local culture, discover new products, and embrace a different way of life. Here are some tips to enhance your shopping experiences:

- **Embrace the Market Culture:** Venture beyond supermarkets and explore the vibrant atmosphere of Bulgarian markets. Engage with vendors, sample local delicacies, and discover the freshest seasonal produce.

- **Support Local Businesses:** Seek out local boutiques, specialty stores, and independent retailers to support Bulgarian businesses and discover unique products.

- **Learn Basic Bulgarian Phrases:** Knowing a few basic Bulgarian phrases related to shopping, such as "How much does this cost?" or "I'll take it," can enhance your interactions and make transactions smoother.

- **Be Open to New Products:** Step outside your comfort zone and explore the diverse range of Bulgarian products on offer. You might discover new favorites and culinary gems.

- **Enjoy the Shopping Experience:** Shopping in Bulgaria is not just about acquiring goods; it's also about immersing yourself in the local culture, interacting with people, and discovering the unique charm of your new home.

CHAPTER TEN: Working in Bulgaria: Job Opportunities, Work Culture, and Taxes

For many expats, finding employment is a crucial step in making Bulgaria their new home. Whether you're seeking new career opportunities, want to supplement your income, or simply wish to immerse yourself in the local work culture, understanding the Bulgarian job market is essential. This chapter explores the intricacies of working in Bulgaria, covering job opportunities, work culture nuances, and the tax implications for expats.

The Bulgarian Job Market: Opportunities and Challenges

Bulgaria's economy has undergone significant transformations since its transition to a market economy in the 1990s. While the country has made strides in developing various sectors, the job market presents both opportunities and challenges for expats.

Key Sectors: Driving Economic Growth

Several key sectors drive Bulgaria's economic growth and offer potential employment opportunities for expats:

- **Information Technology (IT):** Bulgaria has emerged as a regional hub for IT services, software development, and outsourcing, attracting international companies and creating a demand for skilled IT professionals. Expats with experience in software engineering, web development, data analysis, and cybersecurity might find promising opportunities in this thriving sector.

- **Tourism:** With its stunning coastlines, picturesque mountains, historical sites, and affordable prices, Bulgaria's tourism industry continues to grow, creating jobs in hospitality, travel, and related services. Expats with language skills, customer service experience, and a passion for tourism might find fulfilling roles in hotels, restaurants, travel agencies, and tour operators.

- **Manufacturing:** Bulgaria has a long-standing tradition in manufacturing, particularly in the automotive, electronics, and food processing industries. While some manufacturing jobs might require specialized skills, opportunities exist for expats with experience in production, quality control, logistics, and supply chain management.

- **Outsourcing and Business Process Outsourcing (BPO):** Bulgaria has become an attractive destination for outsourcing and BPO services, thanks to its relatively low labor costs, skilled workforce, and multilingual capabilities. Expats with experience in customer service, technical support, data entry, and finance might find opportunities in these growing fields.

Challenges: Competition, Language, and Bureaucracy

Despite the opportunities, the Bulgarian job market also presents challenges for expats:

- **Competition:** The unemployment rate in Bulgaria has declined in recent years, but competition for jobs remains high, especially for entry-level positions. Expats might face competition from local candidates with similar skills and qualifications.

- **Language Barrier:** While English is spoken in some sectors, particularly IT and tourism, fluency in Bulgarian is often a requirement for many jobs, especially those involving interaction with local clients or colleagues.

- **Bureaucracy:** Navigating the work permit and visa processes can be time-consuming and complex for non-EU citizens, requiring meticulous attention to detail and adherence to specific regulations.

Finding a Job in Bulgaria: Exploring Avenues

The job search process in Bulgaria often involves a combination of online platforms, networking, and recruitment agencies. Here are some avenues to explore:

Online Job Portals: Casting a Wide Net

Numerous online job portals cater to the Bulgarian job market, allowing you to browse job listings, filter by industry, location, and keywords, and create job alerts to receive notifications for relevant openings. Popular job portals include:

- **Jobs.bg:** A leading Bulgarian job portal with a wide range of job listings across various sectors.

- **Zaplata.bg:** Another popular job portal offering job listings, company profiles, and career advice.

- **Rabota.bg:** A job portal focused on IT and technical jobs, featuring listings from Bulgarian and international companies.

- **LinkedIn:** A professional networking platform with a growing presence in Bulgaria, allowing you to connect with professionals in your field, explore job opportunities, and showcase your skills and experience.

Networking: Tapping into Personal Connections

Networking plays a crucial role in the Bulgarian job search process. Connect with people in your field, attend industry events, and leverage your personal and professional connections to explore potential opportunities.

- **Expat Communities:** Join expat communities and forums online or in your local area to connect with other expats working in Bulgaria, gain insights into the job market, and share experiences.

- **Industry Events and Conferences:** Attend industry-specific events and conferences to meet potential employers, learn about industry trends, and expand your professional network.

- **Professional Associations:** Join professional associations related to your field to connect with colleagues, access industry resources, and explore job opportunities.

Recruitment Agencies: Professional Assistance and Industry Expertise

Recruitment agencies can provide valuable assistance in your job search, leveraging their industry expertise, network of contacts, and knowledge of the Bulgarian job market.

- **Specialized Agencies:** Some agencies specialize in specific sectors, such as IT, finance, or tourism, providing a more targeted approach to your job search.

- **International Agencies:** International recruitment agencies often have a presence in Bulgaria, connecting international candidates with local employers.

- **Agency Fees:** Be aware that some recruitment agencies might charge fees to candidates or employers, or both. Clarify the agency's fee structure before engaging their services.

Direct Applications: Targeting Specific Companies

If you have specific companies in mind, consider submitting direct applications through their websites or career portals. Research the company's culture, values, and hiring practices to tailor your application and highlight your relevant skills and experience.

Language Proficiency: A Crucial Asset

Fluency in Bulgarian is often a prerequisite for many jobs in Bulgaria, especially those involving interaction with local clients, colleagues, or government agencies. If you're not fluent in Bulgarian, consider language courses or immersion programs to improve your language skills and enhance your job prospects.

Work Culture in Bulgaria: Adapting to Nuances

Bulgaria's work culture reflects its historical, social, and economic context, presenting both similarities and differences compared to other European countries. Understanding these nuances can help you adapt to the Bulgarian work environment and navigate professional interactions effectively.

Hierarchy and Formality: Respecting Authority

Bulgarian work culture often emphasizes hierarchy and formality, with a clear distinction between management and employees. Respect for authority figures and adherence to established protocols are expected.

- **Addressing Colleagues:** Use formal titles and surnames when addressing colleagues, especially those in senior positions, unless invited to use more informal terms.

- **Communication Style:** Communication is generally direct and straightforward, but maintaining a professional and respectful tone is crucial.

- **Decision-Making:** Decision-making processes often involve consultations and approvals from higher-ups, reflecting the hierarchical structure.

Work-Life Balance: Shifting Priorities

While work-life balance is gaining importance in Bulgaria, work commitments often take precedence, with longer working hours and a willingness to go the extra mile being common.

- **Overtime:** Overtime work is not uncommon, especially during busy periods or for urgent projects.

- **Vacation Time:** Employees are typically entitled to 20 days of paid vacation per year, but taking longer vacations might be less common.

- **Socializing with Colleagues:** Socializing with colleagues outside of work is common, fostering team bonding and building relationships.

Communication Style: Directness and Context

Bulgarian communication style is generally direct and to the point, with less emphasis on indirect communication or nuanced expressions. Context plays a significant role in understanding the intended meaning.

- **Nonverbal Communication:** Pay attention to nonverbal cues, such as body language and facial expressions, as they often convey additional meaning.

- **Humor:** Humor is appreciated in the workplace, but avoid sensitive topics or jokes that might be misconstrued.

Building Relationships: Trust and Personal Connections

Building trust and personal connections are crucial in Bulgarian work culture. Investing time in getting to know your colleagues, engaging in social interactions, and demonstrating your commitment to the team can foster stronger working relationships.

Employment Contracts: Understanding Your Rights

Employment contracts in Bulgaria outline the terms and conditions of employment, including salary, working hours, vacation time, and termination procedures. It's essential to carefully review and understand your employment contract before signing it.

Key Provisions: Protecting Your Interests

Key provisions in Bulgarian employment contracts typically include:

- **Job Title and Description:** A clear definition of your job title, responsibilities, and reporting structure.

- **Salary and Benefits:** Your gross salary, payment frequency, and any additional benefits, such as health insurance, transportation allowance, or bonuses.

- **Working Hours:** Your regular working hours, overtime provisions, and breaks.

- **Vacation Time:** Your annual vacation entitlement and procedures for requesting leave.

- **Sick Leave:** Provisions for sick leave, including documentation requirements and payment procedures.

- **Termination Procedures:** Notice periods, grounds for termination, and severance pay entitlements.

Legal Advice: Seeking Professional Guidance

If you have questions or concerns about your employment contract, seek legal advice from a qualified employment lawyer to ensure your rights and interests are protected.

Taxes in Bulgaria: Implications for Expats

As an expat working in Bulgaria, you'll be liable for taxes on your income, depending on your residency status and the source of your income. Bulgaria's tax system is relatively straightforward, with a flat income tax rate of 10%.

Residency Status: Determining Your Tax Obligations

Your residency status determines your tax obligations in Bulgaria. You're considered a tax resident if you:

- **Spend more than 183 days in Bulgaria in a calendar year.**

- **Have your permanent address or center of vital interests in Bulgaria.**

Tax residents are liable for taxes on their worldwide income, while non-residents are only taxed on income earned in Bulgaria.

Income Tax: A Flat Rate of 10%

Bulgaria has a flat income tax rate of 10%, applied to all types of income, including salaries, wages, self-employment income, and investment income.

Social Security Contributions: Shared by Employer and Employee

Social security contributions are shared by employers and employees, covering pensions, healthcare, and unemployment insurance. The rates for social security contributions vary depending on your income and employment status.

Tax Registration: Obtaining a Personal Identification Number (PIN)

To work legally in Bulgaria, you'll need to obtain a personal identification number (PIN) from the National Revenue Agency (NRA). Your PIN is required for tax registration, employment contracts, and other official documents.

Tax Filing: Annual Declarations and Deadlines

Tax residents in Bulgaria are required to file an annual tax return, declaring their worldwide income and any deductions or credits they're eligible for. The deadline for filing tax returns is typically April 30th of the following year.

Tax Advice: Seeking Professional Guidance

Navigating the complexities of tax regulations can be challenging, especially for expats unfamiliar with the Bulgarian tax system. Seeking professional advice from a qualified tax advisor can help you understand your tax obligations, optimize your tax situation, and ensure compliance with Bulgarian tax laws.

Working in Bulgaria: Embracing the Experience

Working in Bulgaria offers a unique opportunity to immerse yourself in the local work culture, expand your professional network, and gain valuable experience in a different economic environment. While challenges exist, a positive attitude, a willingness to learn, and a proactive approach can help you navigate the job market, adapt to the work culture, and achieve professional success in your new Bulgarian home.

CHAPTER ELEVEN: Bulgarian Culture and Etiquette: Customs, Traditions, and Social Norms

Bulgaria, with its rich history and unique cultural heritage, offers a fascinating blend of traditions, customs, and social norms. As an expat, understanding these nuances is crucial for navigating your new environment, building meaningful relationships with locals, and embracing a fulfilling cultural experience. This chapter delves into the intricacies of Bulgarian culture and etiquette, providing you with insights and practical guidance to navigate social interactions with sensitivity and respect.

Bulgarian Hospitality: A Warm Welcome and Generous Spirit

Bulgarians are renowned for their warm hospitality and generous spirit, welcoming guests with open arms and a genuine desire to make them feel at home. Hospitality is deeply ingrained in Bulgarian culture, and you'll likely encounter this warmth and generosity in various social settings.

Home Invitations: A Gesture of Friendship

Receiving an invitation to a Bulgarian home is a special honor, signifying a gesture of friendship and a desire to share their culture and traditions with you. If you're invited to a Bulgarian home, it's customary to bring a small gift, such as flowers, chocolates, or a bottle of wine, as a token of appreciation.

Table Manners: Politeness and Respect

Bulgarian table manners reflect a culture that values politeness and respect. Here are some etiquette tips to keep in mind:

- **Wait for the Host to Invite You to Sit:** Don't sit down at the table until the host invites you to do so.

- **Use Utensils:** Bulgarians typically use utensils for most meals, even for dishes that might be eaten with hands in other cultures.

- **Keep Your Hands Above the Table:** It's considered impolite to rest your elbows on the table or keep your hands below the table during a meal.

- **Don't Start Eating Until Everyone is Served:** Wait for everyone to be served before you begin eating.

- **Compliment the Host on the Food:** Expressing appreciation for the food is a sign of good manners and shows respect for the host's efforts.

- **Finish Your Plate:** It's considered polite to finish everything on your plate, as it shows respect for the food and the host's hospitality.

Toasting Traditions: Cheers to Good Health and Friendship

Toasting is an integral part of Bulgarian social gatherings, symbolizing good health, friendship, and shared moments. When toasting, it's customary to look into the eyes of the person you're toasting with and say "Наздраве!" (Nazdrave!), which means "Cheers!"

Gift-Giving: A Token of Appreciation

Gift-giving is a common practice in Bulgaria, expressing appreciation, gratitude, or celebrating special occasions. When choosing a gift, consider the recipient's interests, preferences, and the occasion. Avoid giving expensive or extravagant gifts, as it might make the recipient feel uncomfortable.

Saying Thank You: Expressing Gratitude

Expressing gratitude is essential in Bulgarian culture, and saying "Благодаря" (Blagodarya), meaning "Thank you," is a common courtesy in various social settings. You can also use more elaborate expressions like "Благодаря ви много" (Blagodarya vi mnogo), meaning "Thank you very much," to convey deeper appreciation.

Communication Style: Directness, Body Language, and Humor

Bulgarian communication style is generally direct and straightforward, with less emphasis on indirect communication or nuanced expressions. Context plays a significant role in understanding the intended meaning, and paying attention to nonverbal cues, such as body language and facial expressions, is crucial.

Direct Communication: Clarity and Honesty

Bulgarians value clarity and honesty in communication, expressing their thoughts and opinions directly, without beating around the bush. While this directness might seem blunt at times, it's not intended to be rude or disrespectful. Embrace this directness and communicate your own thoughts and feelings openly and honestly.

Body Language: Nonverbal Cues and Gestures

Nonverbal communication plays a significant role in Bulgarian interactions, often conveying additional meaning beyond spoken words. Pay attention to body language, facial expressions, and gestures to understand the full context of a conversation.

- **Eye Contact:** Maintaining eye contact during conversations is a sign of respect and engagement.

- **Head Nod:** A nod of the head can indicate agreement or understanding.

- **Hand Gestures:** Bulgarians often use hand gestures to emphasize points or express emotions.

Humor: A Shared Connection

Humor is appreciated in Bulgarian culture, and sharing a laugh can create a sense of connection and camaraderie. However, be mindful of sensitive topics, cultural differences, and jokes that might be misconstrued.

Social Customs: Respect, Tradition, and Superstitions

Bulgaria's social customs reflect its rich history, traditional values, and a blend of folklore and superstitions. Understanding these customs can help you navigate social situations with sensitivity and avoid unintentional faux pas.

Respect for Elders: A Sign of Good Character

Bulgarians have a deep respect for elders, honoring their wisdom, experience, and contributions to society. This respect is manifested in various ways, from addressing elders with formal titles and offering them seats on public transport to seeking their advice and valuing their opinions.

Traditional Values: Family, Community, and Patriotism

Bulgarian culture places a strong emphasis on family, community, and patriotism. Family ties are close-knit, with extended family members often playing a significant role in each other's lives. Community spirit is strong, with neighbors often supporting each other and participating in local events and traditions. Patriotism is also deeply ingrained, with Bulgarians taking pride in their country's history, culture, and achievements.

Superstitions: A Blend of Folklore and Beliefs

Bulgarians have a rich tapestry of folklore and superstitions, some deeply rooted in ancient traditions and beliefs. While not everyone adheres to these superstitions, they are often ingrained in everyday language and customs.

- **Evil Eye:** The belief in the "evil eye," a malevolent gaze that can bring bad luck, is prevalent in Bulgaria. People often wear amulets or charms to ward off the evil eye.

- **Spilling Salt:** Spilling salt is considered bad luck, and it's customary to throw a pinch of salt over your left shoulder to counteract the misfortune.

- **Black Cat Crossing Your Path:** A black cat crossing your path is also considered bad luck. To avoid the misfortune, it's customary to wait for someone else to cross the path first.

- **Knocking on Wood:** Knocking on wood is a common superstition to ward off bad luck or jinxing something good.

Name Days: Celebrating Personal Patron Saints

In addition to birthdays, Bulgarians also celebrate name days, honoring the feast day of the saint associated with their given name. Name days are often celebrated with family gatherings, gifts, and special meals.

Bulgarian Orthodox Christianity: A Cultural Cornerstone

Bulgarian Orthodox Christianity has played a significant role in shaping Bulgarian culture, traditions, and values. While not everyone actively practices the religion, its influence is evident in various aspects of Bulgarian life, from religious holidays and festivals to art, architecture, and social customs.

Religious Holidays: Easter and Christmas

Easter and Christmas are the two most important religious holidays in Bulgaria, celebrated with a blend of religious traditions and festive customs.

- **Easter:** Bulgarian Easter traditions include painting eggs red, symbolizing the blood of Christ, and baking special Easter bread, known as "kozunak."

- **Christmas:** Bulgarian Christmas celebrations typically involve a festive dinner on Christmas Eve, followed by attending church services and exchanging gifts.

Embracing Bulgarian Culture: A Journey of Discovery

As an expat in Bulgaria, embracing the local culture is a journey of discovery, enriching your experience and fostering meaningful connections with the people and the place. Here are some tips to help you navigate this cultural journey:

Learn the Language: Unlocking Cultural Nuances

Learning Bulgarian, even just the basics, demonstrates respect for the local culture and opens doors to deeper connections with Bulgarians. It allows you to understand conversations, participate in social interactions, and appreciate the nuances of Bulgarian humor and expressions.

Explore Cultural Attractions: Museums, Historical Sites, and Festivals

Bulgaria boasts a rich cultural heritage, with numerous museums, historical sites, and festivals showcasing its art, architecture, history, and traditions. Exploring these attractions provides insights into the country's past and present, deepening your understanding of Bulgarian culture.

Engage with Locals: Building Relationships and Understanding

Engage with Bulgarians in everyday life, whether it's at the market, in a cafe, or with neighbors. Show genuine interest in their culture, customs, and perspectives. These interactions can foster meaningful relationships, provide valuable insights, and broaden your understanding of Bulgarian life.

Be Open-Minded and Respectful: Embracing Differences

Embrace an open-minded and respectful attitude towards cultural differences. Avoid making judgments or comparisons based on your own cultural background. Accept that things might be done differently in Bulgaria, and approach these differences with curiosity and a willingness to learn.

Patience and Flexibility: Navigating Cultural Adjustments

Adapting to a new culture takes time and patience. Be prepared for cultural adjustments, misunderstandings, and occasional frustrations. Embrace flexibility, maintain a sense of humor, and celebrate your successes along the way.

Celebrate Your Own Culture: Sharing Traditions and Perspectives

While embracing Bulgarian culture is essential, don't forget to celebrate your own cultural heritage. Share your traditions, customs, and perspectives with Bulgarians, fostering cultural exchange and mutual understanding.

Bulgarian culture is a tapestry woven with rich traditions, warm hospitality, and a unique blend of customs and beliefs. As you navigate your new environment, embrace these nuances with an open mind, a respectful heart, and a willingness to learn. The journey of cultural immersion will enrich your expat experience, creating lasting memories and meaningful connections with the people and the place you now call home.

CHAPTER TWELVE: Making Friends and Connecting: Building a Social Life in Bulgaria

Moving to a new country, while exciting, can also feel isolating, especially in the initial stages. Building a social life is crucial for a fulfilling expat experience, fostering a sense of belonging, creating support networks, and enhancing your understanding of Bulgarian culture and society. This chapter explores various ways to make friends, connect with people, and build a vibrant social life in Bulgaria, helping you integrate into your new community and make the most of your time in this welcoming Balkan nation.

Embracing Bulgarian Hospitality: Openness and Warmth

Bulgarians are renowned for their warm hospitality and welcoming nature, often extending a helping hand to newcomers and making them feel at ease. This openness and generosity can be a great starting point for building social connections. Embrace opportunities to interact with Bulgarians in everyday situations, whether it's at the market, in a cafe, or with neighbors. A simple smile, a friendly greeting, or a willingness to engage in conversation can open doors to unexpected friendships.

Language Learning: A Bridge to Connection

Learning Bulgarian, even just the basics, demonstrates respect for the local culture and goes a long way in building rapport with Bulgarians. It shows that you're making an effort to integrate into their society and are genuinely interested in connecting with them. A simple "Здравейте" (Zdraveйte), meaning "Hello," or "Благодаря" (Blagodarya), meaning "Thank you," can spark a conversation and create a positive impression. As your language skills improve, you'll be able to engage in more meaningful conversations, deepening your understanding of Bulgarian culture and fostering stronger connections.

Expat Communities: Shared Experiences and Support Networks

Connecting with other expats can provide a sense of camaraderie and a support network during your initial adjustment to life in Bulgaria. Expat communities offer a platform to share experiences, exchange tips, and navigate the challenges of settling into a new country. They also provide a social outlet, with organized events, activities, and gatherings creating opportunities to meet like-minded individuals from diverse backgrounds.

Online Forums and Groups: Virtual Connections and Information Sharing

Online forums and groups dedicated to expats in Bulgaria offer a virtual space to connect with others, seek advice, and share experiences. These platforms often feature discussions on various topics, from visa and residency issues to finding housing, schools, and healthcare providers. They also provide a platform to ask questions, share recommendations, and connect with people in your local area.

Social Media Groups: Connecting Locally and Discovering Events

Social media groups, particularly Facebook groups, are a popular way for expats to connect locally, discover events, and share information. Many towns and cities have dedicated expat groups, featuring posts about upcoming events, social gatherings, recommendations for local businesses, and discussions on various aspects of expat life.

Expat Organizations and Clubs: Structured Activities and Networking Opportunities

Expat organizations and clubs offer more structured activities and networking opportunities, often organizing events like language exchanges, cultural excursions, social gatherings, and charity initiatives. These organizations provide a platform to meet people with shared interests, expand your social circle, and contribute to your new community.

Local Activities and Interests: Connecting through Shared Passions

Participating in local activities and pursuing your interests is a great way to connect with Bulgarians and expats who share your passions. Whether it's joining a sports club, attending a language class, volunteering for a local organization, or exploring cultural attractions, these activities provide opportunities to meet people, build friendships, and integrate into your new community.

Sports Clubs: Teamwork, Fitness, and Social Bonds

Joining a sports club, whether it's football, volleyball, basketball, tennis, or swimming, offers a chance to stay active, improve your fitness, and connect with people who share your passion for sports. Sports clubs often organize social events and outings, fostering team spirit and camaraderie.

Language Classes: Learning Together and Cultural Exchange

Attending Bulgarian language classes provides a structured environment to learn the language, meet other students, and engage in cultural exchange. Language classes often involve group activities, discussions, and cultural excursions, creating opportunities to connect with fellow learners and practice your language skills in real-life situations.

Volunteer Organizations: Giving Back and Making a Difference

Volunteering for a local organization, whether it's a charity, environmental group, or community initiative, is a rewarding way to give back to your new community, make a difference, and connect with people who share your values. Volunteering offers opportunities to meet like-minded individuals, learn about local issues, and contribute to positive change.

Cultural Attractions and Events: Exploring Together and Sharing Experiences

Bulgaria boasts a rich cultural heritage, with numerous museums, historical sites, theaters, art galleries, and festivals showcasing its art, architecture, history, and traditions. Exploring these attractions and attending cultural events provides opportunities to meet people, engage in conversations, and share experiences, fostering connections through a shared appreciation for Bulgarian culture.

Social Etiquette: Navigating Interactions with Sensitivity

While Bulgarians are generally warm and welcoming, understanding social etiquette nuances can enhance your interactions and prevent unintentional faux pas.

Greetings: Formality and Respect

Bulgarians typically greet each other with a handshake and a verbal greeting. When meeting someone for the first time, it's customary to use formal titles and surnames, unless invited to use more informal terms. Maintain eye contact during greetings, as it conveys respect and engagement.

Personal Space: A Bit Closer Than in Some Cultures

Bulgarians tend to stand a bit closer during conversations than in some other cultures. Don't be alarmed if someone stands closer than you're accustomed to; it's not intended to be intrusive but rather reflects a cultural difference in personal space.

Gestures: Understanding Nonverbal Cues

Bulgarians often use hand gestures to emphasize points or express emotions. Pay attention to these nonverbal cues, as they can convey additional meaning beyond spoken words. For example, a nod of the head can indicate agreement or understanding, while a shake of the head can signal disagreement or confusion.

Gifts: A Token of Appreciation or Celebration

Gift-giving is a common practice in Bulgaria, expressing appreciation, gratitude, or celebrating special occasions. When choosing a gift, consider the recipient's interests, preferences, and the occasion. Avoid giving expensive or extravagant gifts, as it might make the recipient feel uncomfortable. A small, thoughtful gift, such as flowers, chocolates, or a local souvenir, is usually appreciated.

Dining Etiquette: Politeness and Respect

Bulgarian table manners reflect a culture that values politeness and respect. Wait for the host to invite you to sit before taking your place at the table. Use utensils for most meals, keep your hands above the table, and avoid starting to eat until everyone is served. Compliment the host on the food and finish everything on your plate as a sign of appreciation.

Alcohol Consumption: Moderation and Toasting Traditions

Alcohol, particularly rakia, a traditional fruit brandy, plays a role in Bulgarian social gatherings. However, excessive drinking is generally frowned upon, and moderation is key. Toasting is a common tradition, and it's customary to look into the eyes of the person you're toasting with and say "Наздраве!" (Nazdrave!), meaning "Cheers!"

Building Meaningful Connections: Time, Effort, and Authenticity

Building meaningful connections in Bulgaria, like anywhere else, takes time, effort, and authenticity. Be yourself, be open to new experiences, and engage with people genuinely. Don't be afraid to initiate conversations, ask questions, and share your own experiences. The connections you build will enrich your expat experience, creating a sense of belonging, support network, and lasting memories.

Tips for Building a Social Life: Proactive Steps and Openness

Here are some additional tips for building a social life in Bulgaria:

- **Be Proactive:** Don't wait for invitations; take the initiative to reach out to people, invite them for coffee, or suggest activities.

- **Attend Local Events:** Check local event listings, community boards, and social media groups for events, festivals, and gatherings in your area.

- **Join Clubs and Organizations:** Explore clubs and organizations related to your interests, hobbies, or professional field.

- **Volunteer:** Give back to your community by volunteering for a local organization or charity.

- **Be Open to New Experiences:** Embrace opportunities to try new things, explore different parts of Bulgaria, and step outside your comfort zone.

- **Be Patient and Persistent:** Building a social life takes time and effort. Don't get discouraged if it doesn't happen overnight. Be patient, persistent, and keep putting yourself out there.

Building a social life in Bulgaria is a rewarding journey that enhances your expat experience, fostering connections, creating a sense of belonging, and deepening your understanding of Bulgarian culture and society. Embrace the warmth of Bulgarian hospitality, learn the language, connect with other expats, and engage in local activities to build a vibrant social network and make the most of your time in this welcoming Balkan nation.

CHAPTER THIRTEEN: Exploring Bulgaria's History: Ancient Sites, Medieval Wonders, and Ottoman Legacy

Bulgaria's history stretches back millennia, leaving behind a rich tapestry of ancient sites, medieval wonders, and remnants of Ottoman rule. Exploring these historical treasures offers a captivating journey through time, providing insights into the country's cultural heritage, the rise and fall of empires, and the enduring spirit of the Bulgarian people. This chapter delves into some of Bulgaria's most significant historical sites, guiding you through their significance and offering glimpses into the fascinating stories they hold.

Ancient Thracian Heritage: Mysteries of a Lost Civilization

The Thracians, an ancient Indo-European people, inhabited the lands of present-day Bulgaria and surrounding regions for centuries, leaving behind a legacy of enigmatic tombs, intricate gold artifacts, and a rich mythology that continues to captivate historians and archaeologists.

The Valley of the Thracian Kings: A Realm of Royal Tombs

The Valley of the Thracian Kings, located in central Bulgaria, is home to numerous Thracian tombs, dating back to the 4th and 3rd centuries BC. These tombs, often elaborately decorated with murals and carvings, provide insights into Thracian burial practices, religious beliefs, and artistic expressions.

- **The Kazanlak Tomb:** Discovered in 1944, the Kazanlak Tomb is a UNESCO World Heritage Site, renowned for its remarkably well-preserved frescoes depicting Thracian rituals, banquets, and scenes from the afterlife. The tomb's vivid colors and intricate details offer a glimpse into the artistic mastery of the Thracians. Due to its fragility, the original tomb is closed to the public, but an exact replica has been constructed nearby, allowing visitors to experience the tomb's splendor.

- **The Sveshtari Tomb:** Another UNESCO World Heritage Site, the Sveshtari Tomb, dating back to the 3rd century BC, is a masterpiece of Thracian architecture and art. The tomb's unique architectural design features a domed ceiling supported by ten female figures, known as caryatids, with intricately carved faces and elaborate hairstyles. The tomb's murals depict scenes from Thracian mythology, including the deification of the deceased ruler.

The Panagyurishte Treasure: A Golden Legacy

The Panagyurishte Treasure, discovered in 1949 near the town of Panagyurishte, is a collection of nine gold vessels, weighing over six kilograms, dating back to the 4th century BC. The treasure, believed to have belonged to a Thracian king, is a testament to the Thracians' mastery of goldsmithing. The vessels, intricately decorated with scenes from Thracian mythology and daily life, are considered some of the finest examples of Thracian art. The treasure is displayed at the National Archaeological Museum in Sofia, offering a glimpse into the opulence and artistry of the Thracian civilization.

Roman Rule: Remnants of an Empire

The Roman Empire extended its reach into the Balkan Peninsula in the 1st century BC, conquering the Thracian lands and establishing a lasting presence that shaped Bulgaria's history and cultural development. Roman rule brought about significant changes, including the introduction of Roman law, administration, and infrastructure, as well as the spread of Roman culture and language.

The Ancient City of Plovdiv: A Roman Legacy

Plovdiv, Bulgaria's second-largest city, boasts a rich history dating back to Thracian times, but it was under Roman rule that the city flourished as a major urban center, known as Philippopolis. Remnants of Roman architecture and infrastructure are scattered throughout the city, offering glimpses into its Roman past.

- **The Roman Theater:** One of the best-preserved Roman theaters in the world, the Plovdiv Roman Theater, dating back to the 2nd century AD, stands as a testament to the city's Roman heritage. The theater, with its impressive seating capacity of up to 7,000 spectators, once hosted gladiatorial combats, theatrical performances, and public gatherings. Today, the theater is a popular venue for concerts, festivals, and cultural events.

- **The Roman Stadium:** Another impressive Roman structure, the Plovdiv Roman Stadium, dating back to the 2nd century AD, was once the center of athletic competitions and public spectacles. The stadium, with its elongated shape and seating capacity of up to 30,000 spectators, is partially excavated and open to the public, offering a glimpse into the scale and grandeur of Roman entertainment.

- **The Roman Forum:** The Plovdiv Roman Forum, once the heart of the city's political, social, and economic life, was a bustling marketplace, administrative center, and religious hub. Remnants of the forum's structures, including temples, basilicas, and shops, are still visible today, offering insights into the city's Roman urban planning and architectural style.

The Ancient City of Nicopolis ad Istrum: A Roman Outpost

Nicopolis ad Istrum, located near the town of Veliko Tarnovo, was a Roman city founded by Emperor Trajan in the 2nd century AD to commemorate his victory over the Dacians. The city, strategically located on a major Roman road, served as a military outpost, administrative center, and commercial hub.

Excavations at Nicopolis ad Istrum have revealed remnants of Roman houses, shops, public baths, a theater, and a forum, offering insights into the daily life and urban planning of a Roman city in the Balkan provinces. The site is open to the public, providing a glimpse into Bulgaria's Roman past.

The First Bulgarian Empire: A Golden Age of Slavic Culture

The First Bulgarian Empire, established in the 7th century AD, marked a pivotal period in Bulgarian history, ushering in a golden age of Slavic culture and laying the foundation for Bulgaria's national identity. The empire, spanning vast territories across the Balkan Peninsula, emerged as a major power, rivaling the Byzantine Empire and influencing the development of Slavic literature, language, and religion.

The Madara Rider: An Enigmatic Rock Relief

The Madara Rider, a UNESCO World Heritage Site, is an enigmatic rock relief carved into a sheer cliff face near the village of Madara. The relief, dating back to the 8th century AD, depicts a majestic horseman, believed to represent a Bulgarian ruler, spearing a lion. The relief's symbolism and inscription, written in Greek, offer valuable insights into the early Bulgarian state, its rulers, and its cultural influences.

The Ancient Capitals of Pliska and Preslav: Centers of Power and Culture

Pliska and Preslav, the first two capitals of the First Bulgarian Empire, were centers of power, culture, and architectural innovation. These cities, flourishing during the 9th and 10th centuries AD, housed grand palaces, churches, monasteries, and workshops, reflecting the empire's prosperity and artistic achievements.

- **Pliska:** The first capital of the First Bulgarian Empire, Pliska, was a fortified city with an impressive network of walls, gates, and palaces. Excavations have revealed remnants of the Great Basilica, one of the largest churches in medieval Europe, as well as the Throne Palace, a complex of buildings that served as the seat of the Bulgarian rulers.

- **Preslav:** The second capital of the First Bulgarian Empire, Preslav, was renowned for its architectural splendor and cultural vibrancy. The city's Round Church, with its unique circular design and intricate decorations, is a testament to the architectural innovation of the period. Preslav was also a center of literary and artistic activity, home to the Preslav Literary School, which played a crucial role in the development of the Cyrillic script and Slavic literature.

The Rila Monastery: A Spiritual Sanctuary

The Rila Monastery, a UNESCO World Heritage Site, is the largest and most revered monastery in Bulgaria, founded in the 10th century AD by Saint John of Rila, Bulgaria's patron saint. The monastery, nestled amidst the Rila Mountains, has served as a spiritual sanctuary, center of learning, and symbol of Bulgarian national identity for centuries.

The monastery's architectural complex features a stunning array of churches, chapels, residential buildings, and a museum, reflecting a blend of architectural styles and artistic influences. The monastery's main church, dedicated to the Nativity of the Virgin Mary, houses a remarkable collection of frescoes, icons, and woodcarvings, showcasing the artistry of Bulgarian iconography.

The Second Bulgarian Empire: A Revival of Power and Glory

The Second Bulgarian Empire, established in the 12th century AD, marked a revival of Bulgarian power and glory, reclaiming lost territories and reasserting Bulgaria's influence in the Balkan region. The empire, with its capital at Veliko Tarnovo, flourished during the 13th and 14th centuries AD, witnessing a period of political stability, economic prosperity, and cultural revival.

Veliko Tarnovo: The Medieval Capital

Veliko Tarnovo, nestled amidst the picturesque hills of northern Bulgaria, served as the capital of the Second Bulgarian Empire, becoming a thriving center of political, economic, and cultural life. The city's strategic location, fortified walls, and imposing Tsarevets Fortress, perched atop a hill overlooking the Yantra River, made it an impregnable stronghold.

- **Tsarevets Fortress:** The Tsarevets Fortress, once the seat of the Bulgarian emperors, is a testament to the empire's military might and architectural prowess. The fortress's massive walls, towers, gates, and palaces evoke a sense of grandeur and power. Excavations within the fortress have revealed remnants of the Royal Palace, the Patriarchal Cathedral, and numerous churches and residential buildings, offering insights into the life and times of the medieval Bulgarian rulers.

- **Trapezitsa Fortress:** Another imposing fortress, Trapezitsa, located on a hill opposite Tsarevets, served as a religious and administrative center. The fortress housed numerous churches, monasteries, and workshops, reflecting the city's spiritual and economic vitality.

- **The Church of the Forty Holy Martyrs:** The Church of the Forty Holy Martyrs, built in the 13th century AD, commemorates the forty Roman soldiers who were martyred for their Christian faith. The church, with its impressive architecture and historical significance, houses the tombs of several Bulgarian emperors and serves as a symbol of Bulgarian national pride.

The Ottoman Legacy: A Period of Transformation

The Ottoman Empire conquered Bulgaria in the late 14th century AD, ushering in a period of profound transformation that lasted for nearly five centuries. Ottoman rule brought about significant changes in Bulgaria's social, economic, and religious landscape, leaving behind a legacy that is still visible today.

Architectural Influences: Mosques, Bridges, and Baths

Ottoman architecture left its mark on Bulgaria, with mosques, bridges, and public baths becoming prominent features in many towns and cities. These structures, often characterized by their domes, minarets, and intricate decorations, reflect the Ottoman Empire's architectural style and its influence on Bulgarian urban landscapes.

- **The Banya Bashi Mosque in Sofia:** The Banya Bashi Mosque, built in the 16th century AD, is one of the few remaining Ottoman mosques in Sofia. The mosque, with its distinctive dome and minaret, stands as a reminder of the city's Ottoman past.

- **The Covered Bridge in Lovech:** The Covered Bridge in Lovech, built in the 19th century AD, is a unique Ottoman-era structure that spans the Osam River. The bridge, with its wooden construction and covered walkway, was once a bustling marketplace and a vital link between the two parts of the city.

Cultural Blending: Culinary Traditions and Language

Ottoman rule also influenced Bulgarian cuisine, introducing new ingredients, spices, and cooking techniques. Turkish coffee, baklava, and other Ottoman delicacies became part of Bulgarian culinary traditions. The Bulgarian language also incorporated Turkish words and phrases, reflecting the cultural blending that occurred during this period.

Exploring Bulgaria's History: A Journey Through Time

Immersing yourself in Bulgaria's history is a captivating journey through time, offering insights into the country's cultural heritage, the rise and fall of empires, and the resilience of the Bulgarian people. Here are some tips for exploring Bulgaria's historical treasures:

- **Visit Museums and Historical Sites:** Bulgaria boasts numerous museums and historical sites, showcasing its archaeological discoveries, ancient artifacts, medieval architecture, and Ottoman legacy. These institutions offer guided tours, exhibitions, and educational programs that bring history to life.

- **Attend Cultural Festivals and Events:** Many towns and cities host cultural festivals and events throughout the year, celebrating historical events, traditional crafts, and folk customs, providing immersive experiences that connect you to Bulgaria's past.

- **Engage with Local Guides and Historians:** Local guides and historians possess a wealth of knowledge about Bulgaria's history, offering insights, stories, and perspectives that enhance your understanding and appreciation.

- **Read Books and Articles:** Expand your knowledge of Bulgarian history through books, articles, and online resources. These sources provide detailed accounts, historical analyses, and captivating narratives that transport you to different eras.

- **Be Respectful of Historical Sites:** When visiting historical sites, be respectful of the environment, follow guidelines, and avoid touching or damaging artifacts or structures. These sites are valuable cultural treasures that should be preserved for future generations.

Bulgaria's history is a tapestry woven with ancient mysteries, medieval grandeur, and Ottoman influences, creating a captivating narrative that unfolds as you explore its historical sites, engage with its people, and delve into its cultural heritage. Embracing this journey through time will enrich your expat experience, deepening your connection to Bulgaria and providing a profound appreciation for the country's fascinating past.

CHAPTER FOURTEEN: Bulgaria's Natural Beauty: Mountains, Coastlines, and National Parks

Beyond its rich history and vibrant culture, Bulgaria is a country blessed with stunning natural beauty. From towering mountain ranges to picturesque coastlines and verdant national parks, Bulgaria offers a diverse landscape that caters to a wide range of outdoor pursuits and nature enthusiasts. This chapter explores the captivating natural wonders that await you in Bulgaria, providing glimpses into its diverse ecosystems, unique flora and fauna, and the abundance of opportunities for outdoor adventures and tranquil escapes.

Majestic Mountains: A Haven for Hikers, Skiers, and Nature Lovers

Bulgaria's mountain ranges, spanning a significant portion of the country, are a haven for hikers, skiers, nature lovers, and those seeking breathtaking vistas and invigorating fresh air. These majestic peaks, with their rugged slopes, verdant forests, and alpine meadows, offer a diverse landscape for outdoor adventures and tranquil escapes.

The Rila Mountains: Bulgaria's Highest Peak and Glacial Lakes

The Rila Mountains, home to Bulgaria's highest peak, Musala (2,925 meters), are a stunning mountain range in southwestern Bulgaria, renowned for their glacial lakes, cascading waterfalls, and dense pine forests. These mountains, a hiker's paradise, offer a network of well-maintained trails, ranging from leisurely walks to challenging climbs, catering to various fitness levels and experience.

- **Musala Peak:** Ascending to the summit of Musala Peak is a challenging but rewarding trek, offering panoramic views of the surrounding mountain ranges and the vast expanse of the Bulgarian landscape. The climb typically takes two days, with overnight stays at mountain huts along the route. Proper preparation, hiking gear, and acclimatization to the altitude are essential for a safe and enjoyable ascent.

- **The Seven Rila Lakes:** The Seven Rila Lakes, a series of glacial lakes nestled in a picturesque cirque, are a popular destination for hikers and nature lovers. The lakes, named after their shapes and characteristics, offer breathtaking views, crystal-clear waters, and a serene atmosphere. A chairlift provides access to the lower lakes, making them accessible to a wider range of visitors.

The Pirin Mountains: Rugged Peaks and Limestone Scenery

The Pirin Mountains, a UNESCO World Heritage Site, are a rugged and awe-inspiring mountain range in southwestern Bulgaria, characterized by their sharp peaks, jagged ridges, limestone cliffs, and glacial lakes. These mountains, a magnet for experienced hikers and climbers, offer challenging trails, stunning scenery, and a sense of adventure.

- **Vihren Peak:** The highest peak in the Pirin Mountains, Vihren Peak (2,914 meters), is a challenging climb that requires technical skills and experience. The ascent typically involves traversing rocky terrain, navigating steep slopes, and using ropes and harnesses for safety. Proper equipment, training, and a qualified guide are essential for attempting this climb.

- **The Koncheto Ridge:** The Koncheto Ridge, a narrow and exposed ridge connecting two peaks in the Pirin Mountains, is a thrilling hike for experienced adventurers. The ridge, with its sheer drops on both sides, requires a head for heights and careful footing. The views from the ridge are breathtaking, offering panoramic vistas of the surrounding peaks and valleys.

The Rhodope Mountains: Mythology, Folklore, and Gentle Slopes

The Rhodope Mountains, spanning a vast area in southern Bulgaria, are a mountain range steeped in mythology and folklore, known for their gentle slopes, verdant forests, and charming villages. These mountains, a haven for hikers, mountain bikers, and those seeking a more relaxed pace, offer a network of trails, stunning views, and a glimpse into rural Bulgarian life.

- **The Trigrad Gorge:** The Trigrad Gorge, a dramatic limestone gorge carved by the Trigrad River, is a popular destination for hikers and nature enthusiasts. The gorge's towering cliffs, cascading waterfalls, and mysterious caves offer a sense of adventure and awe.

- **The Devil's Throat Cave:** The Devil's Throat Cave, located near the Trigrad Gorge, is a fascinating cave system with an underground river that disappears into a dark abyss, giving rise to legends and myths. A guided tour takes visitors through the cave's chambers, showcasing its unique geological formations and the legend of Orpheus's descent into the underworld.

Mountain Tips: Preparing for Your Adventure

Here are some tips for exploring Bulgaria's majestic mountains:

- **Plan Your Route:** Research trails, check weather conditions, and estimate hiking times to ensure your route aligns with your fitness level, experience, and time constraints. Maps, guidebooks, and online resources provide valuable information for planning your mountain adventures.

- **Pack Essentials:** Bring essential gear, including sturdy hiking boots, layers of clothing for changing weather conditions, a waterproof jacket, a hat, sunscreen, a first-aid kit, plenty of water, and snacks. For more challenging hikes or climbs, consider additional equipment like hiking poles, a headlamp, a map and compass, and a GPS device.

- **Respect the Environment:** Stay on marked trails, avoid disturbing wildlife, pack out all your trash, and respect the natural beauty of the mountains. Follow Leave No Trace principles to minimize your impact on the environment.

- **Be Aware of Weather Conditions:** Mountain weather can change rapidly, so check forecasts before you head out and be prepared for sudden shifts in temperature, wind, and precipitation. Dress in layers, pack rain gear, and be prepared to adjust your plans if necessary.

- **Safety First:** Inform someone about your hiking plans, including your route and expected return time. Carry a whistle, a mirror, and a charged mobile phone for emergencies. If hiking alone, consider joining a guided tour or informing a local park ranger about your route.

Coastal Charms: Sun, Sand, and Black Sea Breezes

Bulgaria's Black Sea coastline, stretching for over 378 kilometers, offers a delightful blend of golden sands, azure waters, bustling resorts, and charming coastal towns. Whether you seek sun-drenched relaxation, water sports adventures, or cultural explorations, Bulgaria's coast offers a diverse landscape for a memorable seaside experience.

Sunny Beach: Bulgaria's Party Hub

Sunny Beach, a vibrant and lively resort town on the southern Black Sea coast, is known for its long sandy beach, bustling nightlife, and abundance of water sports activities. This popular destination attracts a diverse crowd, from families with young children to young adults seeking party vibes.

- **The Beach:** Sunny Beach's main beach, stretching for over eight kilometers, offers ample space for sunbathing, swimming, and building sandcastles. Numerous beach bars, restaurants, and water sports operators line the beach, providing refreshments, entertainment, and rentals for jet skis, paddleboards, and other water toys.

- **Nightlife:** Sunny Beach's nightlife is legendary, with a plethora of bars, clubs, and discos offering a vibrant and energetic atmosphere that extends into the early hours of the morning. Live music, DJs, themed parties, and international crowds create a dynamic and unforgettable nightlife experience.

Golden Sands: Family-Friendly Fun

Golden Sands, a popular resort town on the northern Black Sea coast, is renowned for its long golden beach, family-friendly atmosphere, and lush green surroundings. This destination caters to families with children, offering a variety of activities, entertainment, and accommodations.

- **Aquapolis: A Water Wonderland:** Aquapolis, a large water park located in Golden Sands, provides a day of fun and excitement for all ages. The park features a variety of water slides, pools, wave machines, and other attractions, as well as restaurants, cafes, and shops.

- **Aladzha Monastery: A Rock-Hewn Retreat:** Aladzha Monastery, a rock-hewn monastery dating back to the 14th century, is a fascinating historical site located near Golden Sands. The monastery, carved into a limestone cliff face, features a chapel, monks' cells, and a refectory, offering a glimpse into the monastic life of the past.

Sozopol: History, Charm, and Artistic Vibes

Sozopol, a charming coastal town on the southern Black Sea coast, boasts a rich history dating back to ancient times, with remnants of Greek, Roman, and Byzantine civilizations scattered throughout its old town. This picturesque town, with its cobblestone streets, traditional houses, and artistic atmosphere, offers a blend of history, culture, and seaside charm.

- **The Old Town:** Sozopol's old town, with its narrow streets, wooden houses, and ancient fortifications, is a UNESCO World Heritage Site, preserving the town's architectural heritage and historical character. Explore the winding alleys, admire the traditional houses with their colorful facades, and discover hidden courtyards and charming cafes.

- **The Archaeological Museum:** The Sozopol Archaeological Museum houses a collection of artifacts from the town's ancient past, including Greek pottery, Roman coins, and Byzantine mosaics. The museum's exhibits provide insights into the town's rich history and cultural development.

- **Artistic Atmosphere:** Sozopol is renowned for its artistic atmosphere, with numerous art galleries, workshops, and studios showcasing the works of local and international artists. The town's annual Apollonia Arts Festival, held in late summer, celebrates the arts with concerts, theater performances, film screenings, and exhibitions.

Coastal Tips: Enjoying the Black Sea

Here are some tips for enjoying Bulgaria's Black Sea coast:

- **Choose Your Destination Wisely:** Bulgaria's coast offers a variety of destinations, each with its unique character and appeal. Research different towns and resorts to find one that aligns with your preferences, whether it's lively

113

nightlife, family-friendly activities, historical charm, or tranquil escapes.

- **Book Accommodations in Advance:** During peak season, especially in July and August, coastal accommodations tend to fill up quickly. Book your hotels, apartments, or guesthouses in advance to secure your preferred choice and avoid disappointment.

- **Embrace Water Sports:** Bulgaria's coast offers excellent conditions for water sports, including swimming, sunbathing, surfing, windsurfing, kitesurfing, sailing, and scuba diving. Numerous water sports operators provide rentals, lessons, and excursions.

- **Explore Coastal Towns:** Venture beyond the resorts and explore the charming coastal towns, with their historical sites, traditional architecture, and local flavors. Discover hidden beaches, enjoy seafood delicacies, and experience the authentic charm of coastal Bulgaria.

- **Respect the Environment:** Keep beaches clean, dispose of trash responsibly, and avoid disturbing marine life. Bulgaria's Black Sea coast is a precious natural resource that should be protected and enjoyed responsibly.

National Parks: Preserving Biodiversity and Natural Wonders

Bulgaria has three national parks and eleven nature parks, encompassing diverse ecosystems, unique flora and fauna, and breathtaking landscapes. These protected areas provide havens for nature enthusiasts, offering opportunities for hiking, wildlife observation, and tranquil escapes amidst untouched natural beauty.

Rila National Park: Protecting Bulgaria's Highest Mountains

Rila National Park, Bulgaria's largest national park, encompasses a significant portion of the Rila Mountains, protecting its diverse ecosystems, glacial lakes, cascading waterfalls, and ancient forests. The park, a UNESCO Biosphere Reserve, is home to a variety of wildlife, including brown bears, wolves, chamois, and golden eagles.

- **Hiking Trails:** Rila National Park offers a network of well-maintained hiking trails, ranging from leisurely walks to challenging climbs, catering to various fitness levels and experience. Explore the park's diverse landscapes, discover hidden waterfalls, and admire panoramic views from mountain peaks.

- **Rila Monastery:** The iconic Rila Monastery, nestled amidst the park's forests, is a spiritual sanctuary, historical landmark, and cultural treasure. Visit the monastery, explore its architectural complex, and immerse yourself in its spiritual atmosphere.

Pirin National Park: Preserving Alpine Landscapes

Pirin National Park, a UNESCO World Heritage Site, protects the rugged and awe-inspiring Pirin Mountains, with their sharp peaks, jagged ridges, limestone cliffs, and glacial lakes. The park, home to a variety of endemic plant and animal species, offers stunning scenery, challenging trails, and opportunities for wildlife observation.

- **Vihren Peak:** Ascending to the summit of Vihren Peak, the park's highest peak, is a challenging climb that rewards hikers with breathtaking views of the surrounding alpine landscapes.

- **Bayuvi Dupki - Dzhindzhiritsa Biosphere Reserve:** This reserve, located within Pirin National Park, protects a unique ecosystem with diverse flora and fauna, including old-growth forests, alpine meadows, and endemic plant species.

Central Balkan National Park: Protecting the Heart of Bulgaria

Central Balkan National Park, encompassing a portion of the Balkan Mountains, protects diverse ecosystems, including forests, meadows, rivers, and waterfalls. The park, a haven for wildlife, is home to brown bears, wolves, deer, wild boar, and various bird species.

- **Hiking Trails:** Central Balkan National Park offers a network of well-maintained hiking trails, providing opportunities to explore the park's diverse landscapes, discover hidden waterfalls, and admire panoramic views from mountain peaks.

- **Emen Canyon:** Emen Canyon, a dramatic limestone gorge carved by the Negovanka River, is a popular destination for hikers and nature enthusiasts. The canyon's towering cliffs, cascading waterfalls, and lush vegetation create a breathtaking landscape.

National Park Tips: Enjoying Nature Responsibly

Here are some tips for enjoying Bulgaria's national parks responsibly:

- **Respect Park Regulations:** Follow park regulations, including staying on marked trails, avoiding disturbing wildlife, and refraining from camping outside designated areas.

- **Leave No Trace:** Pack out all your trash, avoid disturbing vegetation, and minimize your impact on the environment.

- **Be Prepared for Changing Weather Conditions:** Mountain weather can be unpredictable, so dress in layers, pack rain gear, and check forecasts before you head out.

- **Inform Someone About Your Plans:** Let someone know your hiking plans, including your route and expected return time, in case of emergencies.

- **Support Conservation Efforts:** Consider donating to or volunteering with organizations that support the preservation and conservation of Bulgaria's national parks.

Bulgaria's natural beauty, encompassing majestic mountains, charming coastlines, and verdant national parks, offers a diverse landscape for outdoor adventures, tranquil escapes, and a deep connection with nature. Embrace the opportunities to explore these natural wonders, respect the environment, and create lasting memories amidst the captivating beauty of this Balkan gem.

CHAPTER FIFTEEN: Festivals and Events: Experiencing Bulgarian Celebrations

Bulgaria's calendar is punctuated by a vibrant array of festivals and events, reflecting its rich cultural heritage, ancient traditions, and a deep connection to the rhythms of nature. From lively folk festivals and colorful religious celebrations to artistic gatherings and contemporary music events, Bulgaria offers a diverse tapestry of experiences that immerse you in the local culture, provide insights into Bulgarian customs, and create unforgettable memories. This chapter explores some of the most notable festivals and events in Bulgaria, inviting you to join the celebrations, embrace the festive spirit, and discover the unique charm of Bulgarian festivities.

Traditional Festivals: Celebrating Heritage and Folklore

Bulgaria's traditional festivals, often rooted in ancient pagan rituals and folklore, celebrate the changing seasons, agricultural cycles, and the country's rich cultural heritage. These festivals, vibrant and colorful, offer a glimpse into Bulgarian customs, music, dance, and culinary traditions.

Kukeri: Chasing Away Evil Spirits with Ritualistic Dance

Kukeri, a traditional Bulgarian ritual, is performed in villages across the country during the winter months, typically around New Year's Eve or Shrove Tuesday. This ancient custom, believed to have pagan origins, involves masked men, known as kukeri, dressed in elaborate costumes adorned with bells, feathers, and animal skins. The kukeri perform ritualistic dances, accompanied by the rhythmic beating of drums and the clanging of bells, to chase away evil spirits, ensure a bountiful harvest, and bring good luck for the coming year.

The kukeri costumes, often representing mythical creatures, animals, or historical figures, are a sight to behold, reflecting the creativity and artistry of Bulgarian folk traditions. The dances, energetic and rhythmic, involve intricate steps, jumps, and gestures, often accompanied by humorous skits and satirical performances that entertain the audience.

Attending a kukeri festival is a unique and unforgettable experience, immersing you in Bulgarian folklore, ancient traditions, and the festive spirit of chasing away winter's darkness and welcoming the promise of spring.

Surva: A Masked Celebration of New Beginnings

Surva, also known as the International Festival of Masquerade Games, is held annually in the town of Pernik, near Sofia, typically in late January. This festival, a UNESCO Intangible Cultural Heritage, celebrates the ancient tradition of survakari, masked performers who roam the streets, performing ritualistic dances and blessings to ensure good health, prosperity, and a bountiful harvest for the coming year.

The survakari costumes, elaborate and often frightening, feature masks carved from wood, adorned with animal horns, feathers, and bells. The masks, representing mythical creatures, animals, or historical figures, reflect the creativity and artistry of Bulgarian folk traditions.

The survakari performances, energetic and rhythmic, involve intricate steps, jumps, and gestures, often accompanied by the rhythmic beating of drums and the clanging of bells. The festival attracts survakari groups from across Bulgaria and neighboring countries, creating a vibrant and colorful spectacle that celebrates the enduring spirit of Bulgarian folklore and the hope for new beginnings.

Nestinarstvo: A Fire-Walking Ritual of Faith and Tradition

Nestinarstvo, a fire-walking ritual practiced in a few villages in southeastern Bulgaria, is a unique and ancient tradition, believed to have Thracian origins. The ritual, performed on the feast day of Saints Constantine and Helena (May 21st), involves barefoot dancing on glowing embers, accompanied by the rhythmic beating of drums and the chanting of prayers.

The nestinari, the fire-walkers, enter a trance-like state before walking on the embers, claiming to be protected from burns by the power of the saints. The ritual, a blend of faith, tradition, and spectacle, attracts locals and visitors alike, witnessing this ancient custom that has been passed down through generations.

Rose Festival: Celebrating Bulgaria's "Liquid Gold"

The Rose Festival, held annually in the town of Kazanlak, in the heart of Bulgaria's Rose Valley, celebrates the blooming of the Rosa damascena, a fragrant rose species used in the production of rose oil, known as Bulgaria's "liquid gold." The festival, held in late May or early June, coincides with the rose harvest season, when the valley is blanketed in a sea of pink and the air is filled with the intoxicating aroma of roses.

The festival's highlights include a rose-picking ceremony, a parade featuring traditional costumes and rose-decorated floats, folk music and dance performances, and a rose queen competition. Visitors can also tour rose distilleries, learn about the rose oil production process, and purchase rose-infused products, such as perfumes, cosmetics, and culinary delights.

The Rose Festival is a vibrant and colorful celebration of Bulgaria's natural beauty, its fragrant heritage, and the enduring spirit of its traditions.

Religious Festivals: Faith, Tradition, and Festive Spirit

Bulgaria's religious festivals, deeply rooted in Bulgarian Orthodox Christianity, blend faith, tradition, and a festive spirit that brings communities together. These celebrations, often marked by religious services, processions, and festive meals, offer insights into Bulgarian religious customs and the cultural significance of faith in Bulgarian society.

Easter: A Celebration of Resurrection and Renewal

Easter, the most important religious holiday in Bulgaria, celebrates the resurrection of Jesus Christ, symbolizing hope, renewal, and the triumph of life over death. Bulgarian Easter traditions blend religious rituals with festive customs, creating a vibrant and meaningful celebration.

- **Holy Week:** The week leading up to Easter, known as Holy Week, is a time for reflection, prayer, and fasting. Churches hold special services, and many Bulgarians observe a strict fast, abstaining from meat, dairy products, and eggs.

- **Good Friday:** Good Friday, the day commemorating the crucifixion of Jesus Christ, is a solemn day of mourning, with churches holding special services and processions.

- **Easter Saturday:** On Easter Saturday, churches hold midnight services, culminating in the proclamation of Christ's resurrection. The priest lights a candle from the Holy Fire, brought from Jerusalem, symbolizing the light of Christ spreading throughout the world.

- **Easter Sunday:** Easter Sunday is a day of joy and celebration, with families gathering for festive meals, exchanging Easter greetings, and breaking the fast with traditional Easter dishes.

- **Red Eggs:** Painting eggs red is a central tradition of Bulgarian Easter, symbolizing the blood of Christ and the renewal of life. The eggs are often decorated with intricate designs and used in traditional Easter games, such as egg tapping, where two people tap their eggs together, and the

121

person whose egg remains unbroken is considered the winner.

- **Kozunak:** Kozunak, a sweet, braided bread, is a staple of Bulgarian Easter celebrations. The bread, often decorated with a red egg in the center, symbolizes the body of Christ and the sweetness of life.

Christmas: A Time for Family, Faith, and Festive Traditions

Christmas, a joyous celebration of the birth of Jesus Christ, is a time for family gatherings, religious observances, and festive traditions in Bulgaria. Bulgarian Christmas celebrations blend religious rituals with a warm and welcoming atmosphere, creating a special time for sharing joy and togetherness.

- **Christmas Eve:** Christmas Eve is a day of preparation and anticipation, with families gathering for a traditional Christmas Eve dinner, consisting of meatless dishes, symbolizing the fasting period leading up to Christmas. The dinner table is often decorated with straw, symbolizing the manger where Jesus was born, and a walnut is placed under each plate, symbolizing good luck for the coming year.

- **Christmas Day:** Christmas Day is a day of celebration and religious observances, with families attending church services and exchanging gifts. A traditional Christmas dinner, featuring roasted meat, banitsa (a savory pastry), and Christmas cookies, is enjoyed in the afternoon.

- **Koledari:** Koledari, groups of young men, roam the streets on Christmas Eve, singing traditional Christmas carols and wishing people good health, prosperity, and a bountiful harvest for the coming year. The koledari are often rewarded with food, money, or small gifts for their performances.

Arts and Culture: Celebrating Creativity and Expression

Bulgaria's arts and culture scene is vibrant and diverse, with numerous festivals and events showcasing the country's artistic talent, musical heritage, and contemporary expressions. These gatherings offer opportunities to immerse yourself in Bulgarian creativity, discover new artistic forms, and engage with artists and performers from Bulgaria and around the world.

Apollonia Arts Festival: A Coastal Celebration of the Arts

The Apollonia Arts Festival, held annually in the charming coastal town of Sozopol, celebrates the arts with a diverse program of concerts, theater performances, film screenings, exhibitions, and literary events. The festival, named after the ancient Greek god Apollo, attracts artists, performers, and audiences from across Bulgaria and internationally, creating a vibrant and eclectic atmosphere.

The festival's program, spanning various genres and disciplines, showcases classical music, jazz, folk music, contemporary dance, theater, film, visual arts, and literature. The festival's venues, including Sozopol's ancient theater, churches, and art galleries, add to the charm and historical significance of the event.

Sofia Film Fest: Showcasing Cinematic Excellence

The Sofia Film Fest, held annually in March, is Bulgaria's largest international film festival, showcasing a diverse selection of feature films, documentaries, short films, and animations from Bulgaria and around the world. The festival attracts filmmakers, actors, producers, and film enthusiasts, creating a platform for cinematic exchange, networking, and the discovery of new talent.

The festival's program, encompassing various genres and themes, offers a glimpse into contemporary cinema, highlighting innovative filmmaking, social commentary, and artistic expression. The festival's screenings, held in various cinemas across Sofia, attract diverse audiences, fostering a shared appreciation for the art of filmmaking.

Spirit of Burgas: A Beachside Music Extravaganza

The Spirit of Burgas, held annually in August, is a large-scale music festival on the Black Sea coast, attracting international music acts and thousands of festival-goers. The festival, known for its diverse lineup, spanning electronic music, rock, pop, and world music, transforms Burgas's central beach into a vibrant and energetic music hub.

The festival's stages, set against the backdrop of the Black Sea, host renowned artists, emerging bands, and local talents, creating an electrifying atmosphere for music lovers. The festival's campsite, located near the beach, provides a communal space for festival-goers to connect, share experiences, and enjoy the vibrant festival atmosphere.

Meadows in the Mountains: A Unique Mountaintop Music Experience

Meadows in the Mountains, held annually in June, is a boutique music festival nestled in the Rhodope Mountains, offering a unique and intimate experience for music lovers seeking a blend of nature, music, and community. The festival, known for its eclectic lineup, spanning electronic music, world music, and experimental sounds, transforms a remote mountaintop village into a magical music haven.

The festival's stages, set amidst the stunning mountain scenery, host international DJs, bands, and performers, creating an unforgettable atmosphere for music discovery and dancing under the stars. The festival's focus on sustainability, community, and artistic expression fosters a unique and welcoming environment for both performers and attendees.

Tips for Experiencing Bulgarian Festivals and Events

Embracing Bulgaria's festivals and events is a rewarding way to immerse yourself in the local culture, discover new artistic expressions, and create unforgettable memories. Here are some tips to enhance your festival experiences:

- **Plan Ahead:** Research festivals and events that align with your interests, check their dates and locations, and book accommodations and transportation in advance, especially if you're traveling during peak season or for popular events. Festival websites, online event calendars, and local tourist offices provide valuable information for planning your festival excursions.

- **Embrace the Festive Spirit:** Bulgarian festivals are often lively and colorful affairs, with music, dance, food, and a welcoming atmosphere. Embrace the festive spirit, join the celebrations, and don't be afraid to participate in traditional dances or customs.

- **Respect Local Customs and Traditions:** Be mindful of local customs and traditions during festivals and events. Dress appropriately, follow etiquette guidelines, and show respect for religious rituals and cultural practices.

- **Learn Basic Bulgarian Phrases:** Knowing a few basic Bulgarian phrases, such as greetings, thank yous, and expressions of appreciation, can enhance your interactions and make transactions smoother.

- **Sample Local Delicacies:** Bulgarian festivals often feature traditional food and drinks, offering an opportunity to sample local delicacies and culinary traditions. Don't hesitate to try new flavors and expand your culinary horizons.

- **Capture Memories:** Bring your camera or smartphone to capture the vibrant colors, festive atmosphere, and unforgettable moments of Bulgarian festivals and events.

- **Be Prepared for Crowds:** Popular festivals and events can attract large crowds, so be prepared for congestion, long lines, and a lively atmosphere. Embrace the energy of the crowd, but also be mindful of personal belongings and safety precautions.

- **Have Fun and Enjoy the Experience:** Bulgarian festivals and events offer a unique opportunity to immerse yourself in the local culture, discover new artistic expressions, and create unforgettable memories. Relax, enjoy the festivities, and embrace the joy of celebrating life in Bulgaria.

Bulgaria's festivals and events are a testament to the country's rich cultural heritage, its vibrant arts scene, and its deep connection to ancient traditions and the rhythms of nature. Embrace the opportunities to experience these celebrations, immerse yourself in the festive spirit, and discover the unique charm and warmth of Bulgarian hospitality. Your participation in these gatherings will enrich your expat experience, create lasting memories, and foster a deeper connection to the cultural tapestry of your new home.

CHAPTER SIXTEEN: Bulgarian Nightlife and Entertainment: Bars, Clubs, and Live Music

Bulgaria might be renowned for its stunning landscapes and rich history, but its vibrant nightlife scene is equally captivating. From cozy pubs tucked away in cobblestone streets to pulsating nightclubs that keep the energy high until dawn, Bulgaria offers a diverse range of options to suit every taste and mood. This chapter explores the after-dark allure of Bulgaria, guiding you through its diverse nightlife offerings, local drinking customs, and the unique atmosphere that makes Bulgarian nightlife so special.

Sofia: The Capital of Nightlife Diversity

As the beating heart of Bulgaria, Sofia boasts a dynamic nightlife scene that caters to every preference. Whether you're seeking a relaxed evening in a traditional Bulgarian pub (mehana), a night of dancing in a trendy club, or live music performances, Sofia has something for everyone.

Mehanas: A Taste of Traditional Bulgarian Hospitality

Mehanas, traditional Bulgarian pubs, are an integral part of Sofia's nightlife, offering a warm and welcoming atmosphere, hearty Bulgarian cuisine, and often live folk music performances. These establishments, usually adorned with rustic wooden decor, embroidered tablecloths, and traditional Bulgarian motifs, provide a glimpse into the heart of Bulgarian culture and hospitality.

At a mehana, expect generous portions of traditional Bulgarian dishes like shopska salad, banitsa, kavarma, and kyufteta, accompanied by a selection of Bulgarian wines, beers, and rakia, the potent fruit brandy. Live folk music performances often feature traditional Bulgarian instruments like the gaida (bagpipe), kaval (flute), and gadulka (fiddle), creating a lively and festive atmosphere.

Trendy Bars and Clubs: Sofia's Cosmopolitan Side

Sofia's trendy bars and clubs cater to a more cosmopolitan crowd, offering stylish interiors, signature cocktails, international DJs, and a variety of music genres, from electronic dance music to hip-hop, R&B, and pop. These establishments, often located in the city center or trendy neighborhoods, attract a mix of locals, expats, and tourists, creating a dynamic and energetic atmosphere.

Some popular areas for trendy bars and clubs in Sofia include:

- **Vitosha Boulevard:** Sofia's main shopping street, Vitosha Boulevard, is lined with upscale bars, cafes, and restaurants, offering a sophisticated and stylish nightlife experience.

- **Studentski Grad:** Known as the "Student City," Studentski Grad is a lively area with a high concentration of students, bars, clubs, and restaurants, creating a youthful and energetic nightlife scene.

- **The Kapana District:** Sofia's Kapana District, a revitalized area with a bohemian vibe, features numerous art galleries, workshops, bars, and restaurants, offering a more alternative and creative nightlife experience.

Live Music Venues: From Jazz to Rock and Everything In Between

Sofia has a thriving live music scene, with numerous venues hosting performances across a wide range of genres, from jazz and blues to rock, pop, and traditional Bulgarian music. These venues, ranging from intimate bars to larger concert halls, provide a platform for local and international musicians, offering a diverse and engaging nightlife experience for music lovers.

Some popular live music venues in Sofia include:

- **Sofia Live Club:** A renowned jazz club that hosts performances by local and international jazz musicians, creating an intimate and atmospheric setting for jazz enthusiasts.

- **Mixtape 5:** A popular club that features a mix of live music performances, DJs, and themed parties, catering to a diverse crowd and a variety of music tastes.

- **Club Terminal 1:** A large concert hall that hosts performances by renowned Bulgarian and international musicians, offering a high-energy experience for fans of live music.

Plovdiv: A Blend of History and Modernity

Plovdiv, Bulgaria's second-largest city and a European Capital of Culture in 2019, boasts a nightlife scene that reflects its blend of history, culture, and modernity. The city's Kapana District, with its cobblestone streets, traditional houses, and artistic atmosphere, has become a hub for trendy bars, cafes, and live music venues.

Kapana District: Plovdiv's Bohemian Heart

Kapana District, Plovdiv's bohemian heart, is a revitalized area that has transformed into a nightlife hotspot, attracting locals, expats, and tourists with its unique charm and eclectic offerings. The district's narrow streets, lined with colorful buildings adorned with street art, create a vibrant and inviting atmosphere.

- **Trendy Bars and Cafes:** Kapana District is home to numerous trendy bars and cafes, offering a variety of drinks, snacks, and atmospheres. From cozy pubs with craft beers and live music to stylish cocktail bars with signature drinks and DJs, Kapana caters to every taste and mood.

- **Live Music Venues:** Live music venues in Kapana host performances across a range of genres, from jazz and blues to rock, pop, and traditional Bulgarian music. The district's intimate bars and open-air stages create a unique and vibrant atmosphere for music discovery and enjoyment.

- **Art Galleries and Workshops:** Kapana District is also a hub for art galleries, workshops, and studios, showcasing the works of local and international artists. Many of these establishments host events, exhibitions, and workshops, adding to the district's creative and cultural vibrancy.

Plovdiv's Historical Charm: Nightlife with a Twist

Beyond Kapana District, Plovdiv's nightlife extends to other parts of the city, offering a blend of historical charm and modern entertainment. Some establishments are housed in traditional Bulgarian houses or historical buildings, creating a unique and atmospheric setting for a night out.

- **Mehanas with a View:** Some mehanas in Plovdiv offer stunning views of the city's landmarks, such as the Roman Theater or the Old Town, providing a picturesque backdrop for a traditional Bulgarian dining experience.

- **Rooftop Bars:** Rooftop bars, offering panoramic city views, have become increasingly popular in Plovdiv, providing a stylish and sophisticated setting for enjoying cocktails, drinks, and the city lights.

- **Cultural Events:** Plovdiv's numerous theaters, concert halls, and cultural centers host a variety of performances, exhibitions, and events throughout the year, adding to the city's cultural vibrancy and providing alternative nightlife options.

Varna: Black Sea Coastline Beats

Varna, Bulgaria's largest city on the Black Sea coast, boasts a vibrant nightlife scene that caters to both locals and the influx of tourists during the summer months. The city's coastal location, with its beautiful beaches and seafront promenades, adds a unique charm to its nightlife offerings.

Beachfront Clubs: Dancing Under the Stars

Varna's beachfront clubs, with their open-air terraces, stunning sea views, and pulsating music, are a magnet for partygoers seeking a high-energy nightlife experience. These establishments, often hosting international DJs, themed parties, and special events, create an electrifying atmosphere that extends into the early hours of the morning.

Some popular beachfront clubs in Varna include:

- **Cubana Beach Club:** A renowned beachfront club with a Cuban theme, offering live music, DJs, cocktails, and a vibrant dance floor, creating a lively and festive atmosphere.

- **PR Club:** A stylish beachfront club with a modern design, hosting international DJs, themed parties, and special events, attracting a trendy and cosmopolitan crowd.

- **Arrogance Music Factory:** A large beachfront club with multiple dance floors, hosting a variety of music genres, from electronic dance music to hip-hop, R&B, and pop, catering to a diverse crowd and a range of music tastes.

Coastal Bars: Relaxed Vibes and Sea Breezes

Varna's coastal bars offer a more relaxed and laid-back atmosphere, perfect for enjoying drinks, snacks, and conversations with friends while taking in the sea views and gentle sea breezes. These establishments, often located on the seafront promenades or tucked away in quiet corners of the city, provide a welcome respite from the bustling crowds and the high-energy clubs.

Live Music Bars: Rock, Pop, and Bulgarian Rhythms

Varna has a vibrant live music scene, with numerous bars hosting performances by local and international musicians. From rock and pop bands to traditional Bulgarian folk music ensembles, Varna's live music bars cater to a variety of music tastes, offering an engaging and entertaining nightlife experience.

Coastal Resorts: Seasonal Nightlife Hotspots

Bulgaria's coastal resorts, particularly Sunny Beach and Golden Sands, transform into nightlife hotspots during the summer months, attracting tourists from across Europe and beyond, seeking sun, sand, and a vibrant party atmosphere.

Sunny Beach: Bulgaria's Party Capital

Sunny Beach, renowned for its long sandy beach and lively nightlife, is Bulgaria's party capital, attracting young adults and partygoers with its plethora of bars, clubs, and discos that pulse with energy throughout the night.

- **Flower Street:** Sunny Beach's Flower Street, lined with bars, clubs, and discos, is the epicenter of its nightlife, offering a vibrant and diverse range of options, from foam parties and karaoke bars to live music venues and themed nightclubs.

- **Cacao Beach: A Beachfront Party Paradise:** Cacao Beach, a beachfront club with a bohemian vibe, hosts international DJs, themed parties, and special events, attracting a trendy and energetic crowd.

Golden Sands: Family-Friendly Fun and Late-Night Entertainment

Golden Sands, while known for its family-friendly atmosphere, also offers a lively nightlife scene, with bars, clubs, and discos catering to a variety of tastes and moods.

- **Party Street:** Golden Sands' Party Street, similar to Sunny Beach's Flower Street, is a hub for bars, clubs, and discos, offering a range of entertainment options, from karaoke bars and live music venues to themed nightclubs and open-air dance floors.

- **The Strip:** The Strip, located near the beach, is another popular nightlife area in Golden Sands, featuring a concentration of bars, clubs, and restaurants, creating a vibrant and energetic atmosphere.

Local Drinking Customs: Cheers to Bulgarian Traditions

Bulgarian drinking customs reflect the country's warm hospitality, social nature, and a love for celebrating life. When enjoying nightlife in Bulgaria, it's helpful to be aware of some local customs:

Rakia: Bulgaria's National Drink

Rakia, a potent fruit brandy, is considered Bulgaria's national drink, often enjoyed as an aperitif or digestif. Rakia is typically made from grapes, plums, apricots, or other fruits, fermented and distilled to produce a strong and flavorful spirit.

Toasting Traditions: Cheers to Good Health and Friendship

Toasting is an integral part of Bulgarian social gatherings, symbolizing good health, friendship, and shared moments. When toasting, it's customary to look into the eyes of the person you're toasting with and say "Наздраве!" (Nazdrave!), which means "Cheers!"

Sharing Drinks: A Gesture of Camaraderie

Sharing drinks with friends and companions is a common gesture of camaraderie in Bulgaria. It's customary to offer drinks to others in your group and to accept drinks offered to you, as a sign of friendship and respect.

Drinking in Moderation: Respecting Social Norms

While Bulgarians enjoy celebrating life and sharing drinks, excessive drinking is generally frowned upon. Drinking in moderation and respecting social norms is important, especially when in public or unfamiliar settings.

Drinking Age: 18 Years Old

The legal drinking age in Bulgaria is 18 years old. Establishments selling alcohol are required to check identification for anyone appearing under the age of 25.

Bulgarian Nightlife: A Unique and Memorable Experience

Bulgaria's nightlife scene, with its blend of traditional Bulgarian hospitality, modern cosmopolitan vibes, and a diverse range of entertainment options, offers a unique and memorable experience for expats and visitors alike. Whether you're seeking a relaxed evening in a mehana, a night of dancing in a trendy club, or live music performances, Bulgaria's after-dark allure is sure to captivate you. Embrace the local drinking customs, engage with the friendly locals, and discover the vibrant energy that makes Bulgarian nightlife so special.

CHAPTER SEVENTEEN: Safety and Security in Bulgaria: Staying Informed and Taking Precautions

Moving to a new country often comes with concerns about safety and security. While Bulgaria is generally a safe country with a low crime rate, it's essential to stay informed about potential risks, take sensible precautions, and understand local safety practices to ensure a secure and worry-free experience. This chapter explores various aspects of safety and security in Bulgaria, providing practical tips and insights to help you navigate your new environment with confidence and awareness.

Personal Safety: Navigating Everyday Life with Awareness

Personal safety in Bulgaria is generally good, with violent crime being relatively rare. However, like in any country, it's essential to exercise caution and awareness, especially in urban areas and crowded places.

Petty Theft: Protecting Your Belongings

Petty theft, such as pickpocketing and bag snatching, can occur in tourist areas, crowded markets, and public transport. Be vigilant, keep your belongings close to you, and avoid displaying expensive jewelry or large amounts of cash.

- **Secure Your Valuables:** Use a money belt or a secure bag to keep your passport, money, and other valuables safe and close to your body.

- **Be Aware of Your Surroundings:** Pay attention to your surroundings, especially in crowded places, and be wary of individuals who might be trying to distract you or get too close.

- **Avoid Leaving Belongings Unattended:** Don't leave your bags, purses, or backpacks unattended in public places, even for a short time.

Scams: Recognizing and Avoiding Common Tricks

Scams targeting tourists and newcomers can occur in Bulgaria, particularly in tourist areas or at transportation hubs. Be wary of individuals approaching you with unsolicited offers, requests for money, or suspicious schemes.

- **Taxi Scams:** Use licensed taxis with working meters, agree on the fare beforehand, and be wary of drivers who take unnecessarily long routes or claim the meter is broken.

- **Money Exchange Scams:** Exchange currency only at reputable banks or exchange bureaus, and avoid individuals offering street-side exchange rates.

- **Distraction Scams:** Be aware of distraction scams, where individuals might try to divert your attention while an accomplice steals your belongings.

Street Safety: Exercising Caution at Night

While Bulgaria is generally safe during the day, exercising caution at night, especially in dimly lit areas or unfamiliar neighborhoods, is advisable.

- **Travel in Groups:** Whenever possible, travel in groups, especially at night, and avoid walking alone in deserted areas.

- **Stay in Well-Lit Areas:** Stick to well-lit streets and avoid shortcuts through dark alleys or parks.

- **Be Aware of Your Surroundings:** Pay attention to your surroundings and trust your instincts. If you feel uncomfortable or unsafe, move to a more populated area or seek assistance.

- **Avoid Excessive Alcohol Consumption:** Excessive alcohol consumption can impair your judgment and make you more vulnerable to crime or accidents. Drink responsibly and be mindful of your surroundings.

Public Transport Safety: Staying Vigilant on Buses and Trains

Public transport in Bulgaria is generally safe, but it's essential to stay vigilant, especially during peak hours when buses and trains can be crowded.

- **Secure Your Belongings:** Keep your bags, purses, or backpacks close to you and avoid displaying expensive items.

- **Be Aware of Pickpockets:** Be wary of pickpockets, especially in crowded areas or when boarding or disembarking.

- **Report Suspicious Activity:** If you notice any suspicious activity or individuals, report it to the driver or a transport official.

Road Safety: Navigating Bulgarian Roads with Caution

Driving in Bulgaria requires adherence to local traffic rules and regulations, awareness of road conditions, and a defensive driving approach.

Road Conditions: A Mix of Modern Highways and Rural Roads

Bulgaria's road network includes modern highways, well-maintained roads, and rural roads with varying conditions. While major highways are generally in good condition, some rural roads might be narrow, winding, or poorly maintained.

- **Plan Your Route:** Research road conditions, especially for rural areas, and choose routes that are well-maintained and suitable for your vehicle.

- **Drive Defensively:** Be prepared for unexpected road conditions, such as potholes, uneven surfaces, or livestock crossing the road.

- **Be Aware of Other Drivers:** Some drivers in Bulgaria might not adhere to traffic rules strictly, so be prepared for unexpected maneuvers and drive defensively.

Traffic Rules and Regulations: Adhering to Local Laws

Adhering to local traffic rules and regulations is crucial for safe driving in Bulgaria.

- **Drive on the Right:** Traffic in Bulgaria drives on the right side of the road.

- **Seat Belts Mandatory:** Wearing seat belts is mandatory for all passengers in the vehicle.

- **Speed Limits:** Speed limits vary depending on the type of road and the area. Generally, the speed limit in built-up areas is 50 km/h (31 mph), on open roads 90 km/h (56 mph), and on highways 140 km/h (87 mph).

- **Blood Alcohol Limit:** The legal blood alcohol limit for drivers is 0.05%. Driving under the influence of alcohol is strictly prohibited and carries severe penalties.

- **Headlights Required:** Headlights must be turned on at all times, even during daylight hours.

- **Winter Tires:** Winter tires are mandatory from November 1st to March 31st, or when road conditions require them.

- **Vignette Required for Highways:** To drive on Bulgarian highways, you need to purchase a vignette, a road toll sticker, available at gas stations, post offices, and border crossings.

Emergency Services: Calling for Assistance

In case of a road accident or emergency, dial 112, the pan-European emergency number, to access ambulance services, police, and fire departments.

- **Provide Your Location:** Be prepared to provide your exact location, including road names or landmarks.

- **Describe the Situation:** Clearly describe the situation, including the nature of the accident, any injuries, and the number of people involved.

- **Stay Calm and Follow Instructions:** Stay calm, follow the instructions of the emergency dispatcher, and provide any necessary assistance.

Road Safety Tips: Staying Safe on Bulgarian Roads

Here are some additional tips for staying safe on Bulgarian roads:

- **Avoid Driving at Night:** Whenever possible, avoid driving at night, especially in rural areas, as road visibility can be poor, and road conditions might be more challenging.

- **Be Cautious in Winter Conditions:** Winter conditions in Bulgaria can be harsh, with snow, ice, and fog affecting road visibility and driving conditions. Drive slowly, use winter tires, and be prepared for potential delays.

- **Be Aware of Wildlife:** Wildlife, such as deer, wild boar, and foxes, can cross roads, especially in rural areas. Be vigilant, especially at dawn and dusk, and reduce your speed in areas with wildlife crossings.

- **Take Breaks on Long Journeys:** On long journeys, take regular breaks to rest, stretch, and stay alert. Fatigue can impair your driving ability and increase the risk of accidents.

Home Security: Protecting Your Residence

Protecting your home from burglary and theft is essential for peace of mind and a sense of security. Taking sensible precautions and implementing security measures can deter potential intruders and safeguard your belongings.

Secure Doors and Windows: Preventing Easy Access

Doors and windows are the most common entry points for burglars, so securing them is crucial.

- **Sturdy Doors:** Ensure your doors are sturdy, with solid frames and secure locks. Consider installing a deadbolt lock for added security.

- **Window Locks:** Install window locks on all windows, especially those easily accessible from the ground or balconies.

- **Security Bars:** In areas with a higher risk of burglary, consider installing security bars on windows or doors for added protection.

Alarm Systems: Deterring Intruders and Alerting Authorities

Alarm systems, both monitored and unmonitored, can deter burglars and alert authorities in case of a break-in.

- **Monitored Alarm Systems:** Monitored alarm systems are connected to a security company, which will notify the police or emergency services in case of an alarm trigger.

- **Unmonitored Alarm Systems:** Unmonitored alarm systems emit a loud siren to deter burglars and alert neighbors, but they don't directly contact authorities.

Surveillance Cameras: Monitoring Your Property and Providing Evidence

Surveillance cameras, both indoor and outdoor, can deter burglars, monitor your property, and provide evidence in case of a break-in.

- **Outdoor Cameras:** Install outdoor cameras to monitor entry points, such as doors, windows, and driveways.

- **Indoor Cameras:** Consider indoor cameras to monitor valuable belongings or areas with limited visibility.

Neighborhood Watch Programs: Community Collaboration for Safety

Participating in neighborhood watch programs, where neighbors collaborate to monitor their community and report suspicious activity, can enhance home security and deter crime.

Home Security Tips: Creating a Safe Environment

Here are some additional tips for creating a safe and secure home environment:

- **Maintain a Well-Lit Exterior:** Install outdoor lighting around your property, especially near entry points, to deter burglars and improve visibility.

- **Trim Shrubs and Trees:** Trim shrubs and trees near windows and doors to prevent burglars from using them as cover.

- **Don't Advertise Your Absence:** Avoid leaving clues that your home is empty, such as overflowing mailboxes, uncollected newspapers, or drawn curtains. Ask a neighbor to collect your mail or newspapers while you're away, and consider using timers to turn lights on and off at specific times.

- **Be Cautious About Sharing Information:** Be cautious about sharing personal information or your home address with strangers, especially on social media.

- **Report Suspicious Activity:** If you notice any suspicious activity or individuals in your neighborhood, report it to the police.

Natural Disasters: Staying Informed and Prepared

Bulgaria is generally a seismically active country, with earthquakes occurring periodically, particularly in certain regions. While major earthquakes are rare, it's essential to be aware of potential risks and take precautions.

Earthquakes: Understanding the Risks and Taking Precautions

Earthquakes, although unpredictable, are a potential risk in Bulgaria.

- **Earthquake-Resistant Construction:** Most buildings in Bulgaria are built to withstand earthquakes, but older structures might be more vulnerable. If you're renting or buying a property, inquire about its earthquake resistance.

- **Earthquake Preparedness:** Create an earthquake preparedness plan, including identifying safe spots in your home, such as under sturdy furniture or in door frames, and having a disaster kit with essential supplies, such as water, food, a first-aid kit, and a flashlight.

- **During an Earthquake:** During an earthquake, drop, cover, and hold on. Stay away from windows, mirrors, and heavy objects that might fall. If you're outdoors, move to an open area away from buildings, trees, and power lines.

- **After an Earthquake:** After an earthquake, check for injuries, evacuate if necessary, and follow official instructions. Be aware of potential aftershocks.

Floods: Seasonal Risks and Precautions

Flooding can occur in Bulgaria, particularly during periods of heavy rain or snowmelt.

- **Flood-Prone Areas:** Be aware of flood-prone areas, especially near rivers and low-lying areas, and avoid driving or walking through flooded streets.

- **Flood Preparedness:** Create a flood preparedness plan, including identifying evacuation routes, having a disaster kit with essential supplies, and securing valuable belongings.

Wildfires: Summer Risks and Precautions

Wildfires can occur in Bulgaria, particularly during the dry summer months.

- **Fire-Prone Areas:** Be aware of fire-prone areas, especially forests and dry grasslands, and avoid activities that might spark a fire, such as smoking or using open flames.

- **Fire Safety:** Follow fire safety guidelines, such as properly extinguishing campfires, avoiding burning trash, and reporting any signs of fire to authorities.

Staying Informed: Accessing Reliable Information

Staying informed about potential risks, safety guidelines, and emergency procedures is crucial for ensuring your security in Bulgaria.

Local News and Media: Keeping Up with Current Events

Local news sources, both in print and online, provide updates on current events, weather forecasts, and any safety alerts or warnings.

Government Websites: Accessing Official Information

Government websites, such as the Ministry of Interior and the National Institute of Meteorology and Hydrology, provide official information on safety regulations, emergency procedures, and weather forecasts.

Embassy or Consulate: Seeking Assistance and Guidance

Your embassy or consulate can provide guidance, support, and emergency assistance in case of a crisis or security incident.

Safety and Security: A Shared Responsibility

Safety and security are a shared responsibility, involving both individual awareness and community collaboration. By staying informed, taking sensible precautions, and supporting community initiatives, you can contribute to a safer and more secure environment for yourself and your fellow expats in Bulgaria.

Remember, while Bulgaria is generally a safe country, exercising caution, awareness, and preparedness can go a long way in ensuring a secure and enjoyable experience. By staying informed, taking sensible precautions, and engaging with the local community, you can navigate your new environment with confidence and peace of mind.

CHAPTER EIGHTEEN: Dealing with Bureaucracy: Tips for Navigating Administrative Processes

Bureaucracy, the intricate web of administrative processes and paperwork, is an unavoidable aspect of life in any country, and Bulgaria is no exception. While the Bulgarian bureaucracy might seem daunting at times, understanding the system, knowing where to go, and being prepared with the necessary documents can make navigating these processes smoother and less stressful. This chapter provides insights and practical tips to help you navigate the Bulgarian bureaucracy effectively, ensuring you have the necessary documentation, permits, and registrations to live, work, and thrive in your new Bulgarian home.

Residency Registration: Establishing Your Legal Presence

Upon arriving in Bulgaria, one of the first administrative tasks you'll need to tackle is residency registration, establishing your legal presence in the country and allowing you to access various services and rights. The residency registration process involves registering your address with the local municipality, obtaining a residency certificate, and, for non-EU citizens, registering your visa or residence permit with the Migration Directorate.

Registering Your Address: The First Step

To register your address, you'll need to visit the municipality office (община - obshtina) in the area where you're residing. You'll need to provide the following documents:

- **Valid Passport or ID Card:** Your valid passport or national ID card, proving your identity.

- **Proof of Address:** A document verifying your address, such as a rental agreement, a property ownership deed, or a notarized statement from your landlord confirming your residency.

- **Visa or Residence Permit (for Non-EU Citizens):** If you're a non-EU citizen, you'll also need to present your visa or residence permit, confirming your legal stay in Bulgaria.

Once you've submitted the necessary documents, the municipality will issue you a residency registration certificate, confirming your registered address. This certificate is essential for various administrative processes, such as opening a bank account, obtaining a Bulgarian driver's license, or registering a car.

Registering Your Visa or Residence Permit (for Non-EU Citizens):

Non-EU citizens with long-term visas or residence permits are required to register their stay with the Migration Directorate (Миграция - Migratsia) within three days of their arrival in Bulgaria. This registration process involves submitting an application form, providing biometric data (fingerprints and photograph), and paying a registration fee.

The Migration Directorate will issue you a registration sticker, which will be affixed to your passport or residence permit, confirming your registered stay in Bulgaria. It's essential to keep your registration up to date, renewing it before its expiry, to avoid potential fines or complications with your residency status.

Obtaining a Bulgarian Driver's License: Navigating the Process

If you plan to drive in Bulgaria, you'll need to obtain a Bulgarian driver's license, either by exchanging your existing foreign driver's license or by taking driving lessons and passing the Bulgarian driving test.

Exchanging Your Foreign Driver's License: Eligibility and Requirements

Citizens of EU and EEA countries can generally exchange their foreign driver's licenses for a Bulgarian driver's license without taking any additional tests, provided their licenses are valid and meet certain requirements. However, citizens of other countries might need to take driving lessons and pass the Bulgarian driving test.

To exchange your foreign driver's license, you'll need to visit the local traffic police department (KAT - KAT) and provide the following documents:

- **Valid Passport or ID Card:** Your valid passport or national ID card, proving your identity.

- **Residency Registration Certificate:** A residency registration certificate, confirming your registered address in Bulgaria.

- **Foreign Driver's License:** Your original foreign driver's license, which will be retained by the KAT.

- **Medical Certificate:** A medical certificate, confirming your fitness to drive.

- **Application Form:** A completed application form, available at the KAT office.

- **Fee:** A fee for the license exchange process.

Taking Driving Lessons and the Driving Test: The Bulgarian System

If you're not eligible to exchange your foreign driver's license or prefer to take driving lessons in Bulgaria, you'll need to enroll in a driving school and pass the Bulgarian driving test. The driving test consists of a theoretical exam and a practical driving exam.

- **Driving Schools:** Numerous driving schools operate in Bulgaria, offering driving lessons, theoretical instruction, and practical training. Choose a reputable driving school with experienced instructors and a good track record.

- **Theoretical Exam:** The theoretical exam tests your knowledge of Bulgarian traffic rules and regulations. You can prepare for the exam by studying the official traffic code book and taking practice tests online or through driving schools.

- **Practical Driving Exam:** The practical driving exam assesses your driving skills, including basic maneuvers, road awareness, and adherence to traffic rules. Your driving instructor will provide guidance and practice sessions to prepare you for the exam.

Bulgarian Driver's License: Validity and Renewal

Once you've passed the driving test, the KAT will issue you a Bulgarian driver's license. Bulgarian driver's licenses are typically valid for 10 years and need to be renewed before their expiry.

Registering a Car: Navigating the Bureaucracy

If you plan to own a car in Bulgaria, you'll need to register it with the local traffic police department (KAT - KAT), obtaining Bulgarian license plates and ensuring your vehicle is legally permitted to drive on Bulgarian roads.

Required Documents: Ensuring a Smooth Registration Process

To register a car in Bulgaria, you'll need to gather the following documents:

- **Valid Passport or ID Card:** Your valid passport or national ID card, proving your identity.

- **Residency Registration Certificate:** A residency registration certificate, confirming your registered address in Bulgaria.

- **Vehicle Registration Certificate:** The original vehicle registration certificate, known as "голям талон" (golyam talon), issued by the previous owner. If you purchased the car new from a dealership, they will typically handle the initial registration process.

- **Technical Inspection Certificate:** A valid technical inspection certificate, confirming the car's roadworthiness. Technical inspections are required annually for most vehicles in Bulgaria.

- **Insurance Policy:** Proof of valid car insurance, including third-party liability coverage, which is mandatory in Bulgaria.

- **Bill of Sale or Purchase Agreement:** A document proving your ownership of the car, such as a bill of sale or a purchase agreement.

- **Customs Declaration (for Imported Cars):** If you imported the car from another country, you'll also need to provide a customs declaration, confirming that all import duties and taxes have been paid.

Registration Process: Steps at the KAT Office

Once you've gathered all the necessary documents, you'll need to visit the local KAT office to register your car. The registration process typically involves:

- **Submitting Documents:** Submitting the required documents to a KAT officer.

- **Vehicle Inspection:** A brief vehicle inspection to verify the car's VIN number and other details.

- **Payment of Fees:** Paying registration fees, which vary depending on the car's age, engine size, and other factors.

- **Issuance of License Plates:** Receiving Bulgarian license plates for your car.

Car Insurance: Mandatory Coverage

Car insurance, including third-party liability coverage, is mandatory in Bulgaria. Third-party liability insurance covers damages or injuries you might cause to other people or their property while driving. You can purchase car insurance from various insurance companies operating in Bulgaria.

Road Tax: Annual Payment

In addition to car insurance, you'll also need to pay an annual road tax, known as "винетка" (vinetka), to drive on Bulgarian highways. Vignettes are available for purchase at gas stations, post offices, and border crossings.

Dealing with Utilities: Setting Up Essential Services

Setting up utilities, such as electricity, water, gas, and internet, is an essential step in settling into your new Bulgarian home. The process typically involves contacting the respective utility providers, providing necessary documentation, and arranging for the installation or activation of services.

Electricity: Energo-Pro and EVN

Two major electricity providers operate in Bulgaria: Energo-Pro, serving northern Bulgaria, and EVN, serving southern Bulgaria. To set up electricity service, you'll need to contact the provider in your area and provide the following documents:

- **Valid Passport or ID Card:** Your valid passport or national ID card, proving your identity.

- **Residency Registration Certificate:** A residency registration certificate, confirming your registered address in Bulgaria.

- **Rental Agreement or Property Ownership Deed:** A document proving your right to occupy the property, such as a rental agreement or a property ownership deed.

- **Meter Reading:** An initial meter reading, if applicable.

Water: Local Water Companies

Water services in Bulgaria are provided by local water companies, which vary depending on the region. To set up water service, you'll need to contact the water company in your area and provide similar documents as those required for electricity service.

Gas: Overgas and Bulgargaz

Two major gas providers operate in Bulgaria: Overgas and Bulgargaz. To set up gas service, you'll need to contact the provider in your area and provide similar documents as those required for electricity and water services.

Internet: A1, Vivacom, and Telenor

Several internet providers operate in Bulgaria, including A1, Vivacom, and Telenor. To set up internet service, you'll need to contact the provider of your choice and provide similar documents as those required for other utilities.

Utility Bills: Payment Methods

Utility bills in Bulgaria can typically be paid online, through bank transfers, at post offices, or at designated payment kiosks. Some utility providers also offer automatic payment options.

Healthcare: Registering with the National Health Insurance Fund

If you're planning to work in Bulgaria or become a long-term resident, you'll need to register with the National Health Insurance Fund (NHIF) to access public healthcare services.

Registration Process: Employer or Individual Registration

If you're employed, your employer will typically handle the registration process and deductions for health insurance contributions. Self-employed individuals or those not covered by employer contributions are responsible for registering with the NHIF directly.

To register with the NHIF, you'll need to visit their office and provide the following documents:

- **Valid Passport or ID Card:** Your valid passport or national ID card, proving your identity.

- **Residency Registration Certificate:** A residency registration certificate, confirming your registered address in Bulgaria.

- **Work Permit or Residence Permit (for Non-EU Citizens):** If you're a non-EU citizen, you'll also need to present your work permit or residence permit, confirming your legal right to work or reside in Bulgaria.

Health Insurance Card: Accessing Healthcare Services

Once you've registered with the NHIF, they will issue you a health insurance card, which entitles you to access public healthcare services, including consultations with general practitioners, specialists, hospitalization, and prescribed medications. Co-payments might apply for some services or medications.

Dealing with Bureaucracy: Tips for a Smoother Experience

Navigating the Bulgarian bureaucracy can be a challenging but manageable process. Here are some tips to make the experience smoother:

- **Gather Documents in Advance:** Before starting any administrative process, gather all the necessary documents, including original documents and photocopies, to avoid unnecessary delays or trips back and forth.

- **Learn Basic Bulgarian Phrases:** Knowing a few basic Bulgarian phrases related to administrative processes, such as greetings, requests for information, and expressions of gratitude, can be helpful when interacting with officials.

- **Be Patient and Persistent:** Bureaucratic processes can sometimes be slow or involve multiple steps. Be patient, persistent, and follow up on your applications or requests if necessary.

- **Seek Assistance if Needed:** If you're struggling to navigate a particular process or encounter language barriers, seek assistance from a Bulgarian-speaking friend, a translator, or a professional consultant who can guide you through the steps.

- **Respect Local Customs:** When interacting with officials, be respectful of local customs, such as addressing people with formal titles and surnames, dressing appropriately, and maintaining a professional demeanor.

- **Stay Informed:** Keep yourself informed about changes in regulations, procedures, or requirements related to administrative processes. Government websites, embassy or consulate websites, and expat forums can provide valuable information.

Embracing the Process: A Part of Expat Life

Dealing with bureaucracy is an inevitable part of expat life, and Bulgaria is no exception. While navigating these processes might require patience and persistence, understanding the system, being prepared, and seeking assistance when needed can make the experience smoother and less stressful. Embracing the process as a part of your Bulgarian adventure will allow you to focus on the more enjoyable aspects of your expat experience, knowing that you have the necessary documentation and permits in place to live, work, and thrive in your new Bulgarian home.

CHAPTER NINETEEN: Cost of Living in Bulgaria: Budgeting for Your New Life

One of the most attractive aspects of moving to Bulgaria for many expats is the relatively low cost of living compared to many Western European countries. However, understanding the actual costs associated with various aspects of life in Bulgaria, from housing and utilities to groceries and transportation, is crucial for creating a realistic budget and ensuring a comfortable and financially sustainable lifestyle. This chapter delves into the intricacies of the cost of living in Bulgaria, providing insights into typical expenses, regional variations, and practical tips for managing your finances wisely.

Housing: Finding Your Affordable Haven

Housing costs in Bulgaria are generally significantly lower than in many Western European countries, offering a wide range of options to suit various budgets and preferences. However, prices can vary depending on factors like location, property type, size, and amenities.

Renting: Affordable Options for Every Budget

Renting an apartment or a house in Bulgaria is generally an affordable option, with monthly rental rates considerably lower than in many other European countries. Rental prices vary depending on location, size, and amenities, with larger cities like Sofia and Plovdiv commanding higher rents than smaller towns or rural areas.

Location	Property Type	Typical Monthly Rent (Leva)
Sofia (City Center)	One-bedroom apartment	800 - 1,500
Sofia (Suburbs)	One-bedroom apartment	500 - 800

Plovdiv (City Center)	One-bedroom apartment	600 - 1,200
Plovdiv (Suburbs)	One-bedroom apartment	400 - 600
Varna (City Center)	One-bedroom apartment	700 - 1,300
Varna (Suburbs)	One-bedroom apartment	500 - 700
Smaller Towns or Rural Areas	One-bedroom apartment	300 - 500

Buying: Investing in Your Bulgarian Home

Buying a property in Bulgaria can be a sound investment, with property prices generally lower than in many other European countries. However, prices can vary significantly depending on location, property type, size, and condition.

Location	Property Type	Typical Price per Square Meter (Leva)
Sofia (City Center)	Apartment	2,000 - 4,000
Sofia (Suburbs)	Apartment	1,500 - 2,500
Plovdiv (City Center)	Apartment	1,500 - 3,000
Plovdiv (Suburbs)	Apartment	1,000 - 1,500
Varna (City Center)	Apartment	1,800 - 3,500
Varna (Suburbs)	Apartment	1,200 - 1,800
Smaller Towns or Rural Areas	House	500 - 1,000

Utilities: Essential Services at Affordable Rates

Utilities in Bulgaria, including electricity, water, gas, and internet, are generally affordable compared to many other European countries. However, actual costs can vary depending on your consumption habits, property size, and the specific utility providers in your area.

Typical Monthly Utility Costs:

Utility	Typical Monthly Cost (Leva)
Electricity	50 - 150
Water	20 - 50
Gas (Heating)	50 - 200 (Winter Months)
Internet	20 - 50

Groceries: Fresh, Local Produce at Reasonable Prices

Groceries in Bulgaria are generally affordable, with fresh, local produce, dairy products, and meats available at reasonable prices, especially at open-air markets (pazars). Supermarkets offer a wider selection of products, including imported goods, but prices might be slightly higher.

Typical Grocery Costs:

Item	Typical Price (Leva)
Bread (Loaf)	1.50 - 2.50
Milk (1 Liter)	2.00 - 3.00
Eggs (10)	3.00 - 5.00
Cheese (1kg)	8.00 - 15.00
Chicken (1kg)	6.00 - 10.00
Beef (1kg)	10.00 - 18.00
Tomatoes (1kg)	2.00 - 4.00
Cucumbers (1kg)	1.50 - 3.00
Onions (1kg)	1.00 - 2.00
Potatoes (1kg)	1.00 - 2.00

Transportation: Getting Around Affordably

Transportation costs in Bulgaria are generally affordable, with public transport being a cost-effective option for getting around cities and towns. Taxis are also relatively affordable, but it's essential to ensure they use a working meter and agree on the fare beforehand to avoid potential scams or overcharging.

Typical Transportation Costs:

Transportation Mode	Typical Cost
Public Transport (Bus, Tram, Trolleybus)	1.60 - 2.00 (Single Ticket)
Taxi (Starting Fare)	0.70 - 1.00
Taxi (Per Kilometer)	0.80 - 1.20
Intercity Bus	Varies depending on distance
Train	Varies depending on distance and class

Dining Out: Enjoyable Meals at Reasonable Prices

Dining out in Bulgaria is generally affordable, with restaurants and cafes offering a wide range of options to suit various budgets and tastes. Traditional Bulgarian restaurants (mehanas) often offer hearty meals at reasonable prices, while more upscale restaurants in larger cities might command higher prices.

Typical Dining Costs:

Dining Option	Typical Cost (Leva)
Meal at a Traditional Bulgarian Restaurant (Mehana)	15 - 30
Meal at a Mid-Range Restaurant	20 - 50
Fast Food Meal	5 - 10
Coffee	2.00 - 4.00
Beer (0.5 Liter)	3.00 - 5.00
Wine (Bottle)	10.00 - 30.00

Entertainment and Leisure: Affordable Options for Every Interest

Entertainment and leisure activities in Bulgaria are generally affordable, with options ranging from free or low-cost activities, such as hiking, visiting parks, or exploring museums, to more expensive options, such as attending concerts, theater performances, or sporting events.

Typical Entertainment Costs:

Activity	Typical Cost (Leva)
Cinema Ticket	10 - 15
Museum Entrance Fee	5 - 10
Theater Ticket	15 - 30
Concert Ticket	Varies depending on artist and venue
Gym Membership (Monthly)	40 - 80

Regional Variations: Cost of Living Across Bulgaria

The cost of living in Bulgaria can vary depending on the region, with larger cities like Sofia, Plovdiv, and Varna generally having higher costs than smaller towns or rural areas. Coastal resorts, particularly during peak season, might also have inflated prices for accommodations, dining, and entertainment.

Sofia: The Capital's Cost of Living

Sofia, as the capital city, generally has a higher cost of living than other parts of Bulgaria, particularly for housing, dining, and entertainment. However, even in Sofia, the cost of living remains relatively affordable compared to many Western European capitals.

Plovdiv: Affordable Charm in a Cultural Hub

Plovdiv, Bulgaria's second-largest city, offers a more affordable cost of living than Sofia, while still providing a vibrant cultural scene, historical attractions, and a charming atmosphere.

Varna: Coastal Living with Seasonal Price Fluctuations

Varna, Bulgaria's largest city on the Black Sea coast, experiences seasonal price fluctuations, with higher costs during the summer months due to the influx of tourists. However, outside of peak season, Varna offers a relatively affordable cost of living, particularly for those seeking a coastal lifestyle.

Smaller Towns and Rural Areas: The Most Affordable Options

Smaller towns and rural areas in Bulgaria generally offer the most affordable cost of living, particularly for housing and groceries. While these areas might have fewer entertainment and leisure options than larger cities, they provide a tranquil and often more authentic Bulgarian experience.

Budgeting Tips: Managing Your Finances Wisely

Managing your finances wisely is crucial for a comfortable and financially sustainable lifestyle in Bulgaria. Here are some practical tips for budgeting effectively:

Track Your Expenses: Understanding Your Spending Patterns

Track your expenses for a few months to understand your spending patterns and identify areas where you might be able to reduce costs. Use a budgeting app, a spreadsheet, or a simple notebook to record your income and expenses.

Prioritize Essential Expenses: Housing, Utilities, and Groceries

Prioritize essential expenses, such as housing, utilities, and groceries, when creating your budget. Allocate a significant portion of your income to these necessities to ensure you can comfortably cover them.

Explore Affordable Options: Markets, Local Shops, and Public Transport

Explore affordable options for groceries, shopping, and transportation. Open-air markets (pazars) offer fresh, local produce at reasonable prices, while local shops might have competitive prices for household goods and services. Public transport is generally a cost-effective alternative to taxis.

Take Advantage of Promotions and Discounts: Saving on Everyday Purchases

Take advantage of promotions, discounts, and sales offered by supermarkets, shops, and restaurants. Many establishments offer loyalty programs or discount cards that can provide additional savings.

Negotiate Prices: A Common Practice in Bulgaria

Bargaining is a common practice in Bulgaria, especially at open-air markets (pazars) and for non-essential items. Don't hesitate to negotiate prices politely, as it's often expected and can result in significant savings.

Live Like a Local: Embrace Bulgarian Customs and Habits

Embrace Bulgarian customs and habits, such as cooking at home more often, enjoying local wines and beers, and exploring free or low-cost entertainment options. Living like a local can help you save money and experience a more authentic Bulgarian lifestyle.

Seek Financial Advice: Managing Investments and Taxes

If you're planning to invest in Bulgaria or have questions about tax implications, seek professional advice from a qualified financial advisor or tax consultant. They can provide guidance and assistance in managing your finances effectively.

Living Affordably: Enjoying the Bulgarian Lifestyle

While Bulgaria offers a relatively low cost of living compared to many Western European countries, it's essential to approach your finances with awareness, planning, and a willingness to embrace local customs and habits. By understanding typical expenses, exploring affordable options, and managing your budget wisely, you can enjoy a comfortable and fulfilling lifestyle in Bulgaria, making the most of your expat experience while staying financially secure.

CHAPTER TWENTY: Bulgarian Property Ownership: Buying or Renting Your Dream Home

Deciding to make Bulgaria your new home often involves finding the perfect place to settle down. Whether you envision yourself in a bustling city apartment, a charming countryside villa, or a cozy mountain retreat, understanding the nuances of property ownership in Bulgaria is essential. This chapter explores the intricacies of buying and renting property in Bulgaria, providing you with the knowledge and guidance to navigate the legal processes, financial considerations, and cultural nuances of the Bulgarian property market.

Navigating the Legal Landscape: Understanding Property Rights

Bulgaria's legal framework regarding property ownership is well-defined, providing clear guidelines for both Bulgarian citizens and foreigners seeking to acquire property. The Bulgarian Constitution guarantees the right to private property, and the country's accession to the European Union has further strengthened property rights and aligned them with EU standards.

Foreign Ownership Rights: Equal Opportunities for Investment

Foreigners, in most cases, enjoy equal rights to Bulgarian citizens when it comes to owning property. However, certain restrictions apply to the ownership of land, particularly agricultural land. Foreign individuals are generally not permitted to purchase agricultural land directly. However, they can establish Bulgarian companies, which are eligible to acquire agricultural land.

Types of Property Ownership: Understanding the Distinctions

Bulgaria's legal framework distinguishes between two primary types of property ownership:

1. **Ownership of the Property:** This type of ownership grants you full rights to the building or structure itself, including the right to use, sell, rent, or renovate the property.

2. **Ownership of the Land:** This type of ownership grants you rights to the land on which the property is built. In some cases, particularly in apartment buildings, you might own the apartment itself but not the land beneath it.

When purchasing property in Bulgaria, it's crucial to understand the type of ownership you're acquiring and the rights associated with it. Review the property deed carefully and seek legal advice to ensure clarity and avoid potential complications.

The Buying Process: Steps to Secure Your Bulgarian Home

Purchasing property in Bulgaria involves a multi-step process, requiring due diligence, legal expertise, and careful financial planning. Here's a step-by-step guide to navigate the buying process effectively:

1. **Finding Your Dream Property:** Begin your property search by exploring various resources, such as real estate agencies, online property portals, and local contacts. Define your criteria, including location, property type, size, budget, and desired amenities, to narrow down your search and focus on properties that align with your preferences.

2. **Engaging a Real Estate Agent:** Working with a reputable real estate agent can streamline the buying process, providing local market knowledge, access to a wider range of properties, and guidance through legal and administrative procedures. Choose an agent with experience working with foreigners and a good

understanding of the legal complexities of property ownership for non-Bulgarian citizens.

3. **Property Viewings and Inspections:** Once you've shortlisted potential properties, schedule viewings to inspect them in person, assess their condition, and evaluate their suitability for your needs. Pay attention to details, ask questions, and consider seeking a professional property inspection to identify potential issues or hidden costs.

4. **Negotiating the Price and Terms:** After finding a property that meets your criteria, negotiate the price and terms of the purchase agreement with the seller. Your real estate agent can assist you in this process, leveraging their expertise and market knowledge to secure a favorable deal.

5. **Preliminary Contract (Предварителен договор):** Once you've agreed on the price and terms, sign a preliminary contract (Предварителен договор), a legally binding document that outlines the essential terms of the sale, including the purchase price, payment schedule, and deadlines for completing the transaction. This contract typically requires a deposit, usually 10% of the purchase price, to secure the property and demonstrate your commitment to the purchase.

6. **Due Diligence: Legal and Financial Checks:** Before finalizing the purchase, conduct thorough due diligence to ensure the property's legal status and financial viability. This process typically involves:

   o **Title Deed Verification:** Verifying the property's ownership through a title deed search, ensuring the seller has the legal right to sell the property and that there are no outstanding claims or encumbrances.

   o **Property Tax Check:** Checking for any outstanding property taxes or other financial obligations associated with the property.

- **Building Permit Verification (for New Properties):** If you're purchasing a new property, verify that all necessary building permits have been obtained and that the construction meets building regulations.

7. **Notary Services: Finalizing the Purchase:** The final step in the buying process involves engaging a notary, a public official who oversees the legal aspects of property transactions. The notary will:

  - **Verify the Documents:** Verify the authenticity of all documents related to the sale, including the title deed, preliminary contract, and proof of payment.

  - **Draft the Deed of Sale:** Draft the deed of sale, a legally binding document that transfers ownership of the property from the seller to the buyer.

  - **Register the Sale:** Register the sale with the Property Register, officially transferring ownership and updating the property's records.

8. **Payment and Transfer of Ownership:** Once the deed of sale is signed and registered, the final payment is made, and ownership of the property is officially transferred to the buyer.

Financial Considerations: Planning Your Property Investment

Purchasing property in Bulgaria involves significant financial considerations, beyond the purchase price itself. Here are some key aspects to consider:

Purchase Costs: Beyond the Price Tag

In addition to the purchase price, various other costs are associated with buying property in Bulgaria:

- **Notary Fees:** Notary fees typically range from 1% to 3% of the purchase price, depending on the property's value and the complexity of the transaction.

- **Property Transfer Tax:** A property transfer tax, usually around 2% to 3% of the purchase price, is levied on property transactions.

- **Legal Fees:** If you engage a lawyer to assist with the purchase process, legal fees might apply, typically a percentage of the purchase price or an hourly rate.

- **Real Estate Agent Fees:** Real estate agent fees are usually paid by the seller, but it's essential to clarify the fee structure and payment arrangements beforehand.

- **Property Taxes:** Annual property taxes are levied on property owners, based on the property's value and location.

- **Insurance:** Property insurance is highly recommended to protect your investment from potential risks, such as fire, theft, or natural disasters.

- **Maintenance Costs:** Ongoing maintenance costs, including repairs, renovations, and utilities, should be factored into your budget.

Financing Options: Mortgages and Loans

Financing options for purchasing property in Bulgaria are available for both Bulgarian citizens and foreigners, with mortgages and loans offered by various banks. However, eligibility criteria, interest rates, and loan terms can vary depending on the lender and your individual circumstances.

- **Mortgage Eligibility:** Mortgage eligibility criteria typically include proof of income, credit history, and residency status. Foreigners might face stricter requirements or higher interest rates compared to Bulgarian citizens.

- **Interest Rates:** Mortgage interest rates in Bulgaria are generally lower than in many Western European countries, but they can fluctuate depending on market conditions and the lender's policies.

- **Loan Terms:** Mortgage loan terms, including repayment periods and loan-to-value ratios, can vary depending on the lender and the type of mortgage.

Currency Considerations: The Bulgarian Lev (BGN)

Property transactions in Bulgaria are typically conducted in Bulgarian leva (BGN). If you're purchasing property with funds in a foreign currency, you'll need to exchange them into leva at a bank or exchange bureau. Be aware of exchange rate fluctuations and any fees or commissions associated with currency exchange transactions.

Renting Property: Flexibility and Affordability

Renting property in Bulgaria offers a flexible and often more affordable alternative to buying, particularly for newcomers who are still exploring different areas or unsure about their long-term plans. The rental market in Bulgaria offers a wide range of options, from apartments and houses to villas and rural properties, catering to various budgets and preferences.

Finding Rental Properties: Exploring Available Options

To find rental properties in Bulgaria, you can explore various resources:

- **Real Estate Agencies:** Real estate agencies specializing in rentals can provide access to a wider range of properties, assist with lease negotiations, and guide you through the rental process.

- **Online Property Portals:** Online property portals, such as imot.bg, olx.bg, and alo.bg, allow you to browse rental listings, filter by criteria, and contact landlords or property managers directly.

- **Local Contacts:** Networking with local contacts, such as friends, colleagues, or expat communities, can lead to off-market rental opportunities or recommendations for reputable landlords.

Rental Agreements: Understanding the Terms and Conditions

Rental agreements in Bulgaria typically outline the terms and conditions of the tenancy, including the rent amount, payment schedule, lease duration, deposit requirements, and responsibilities for maintenance and repairs. It's essential to carefully review and understand the rental agreement before signing it, ensuring clarity on all aspects of the tenancy.

Key Provisions: Protecting Your Rights as a Tenant

Key provisions in Bulgarian rental agreements typically include:

- **Rent Amount and Payment Schedule:** The agreed-upon rent amount, payment frequency (usually monthly), and acceptable payment methods.

- **Lease Duration:** The length of the lease agreement, typically one year, with options for renewal.

- **Deposit:** A security deposit, usually one or two months' rent, is typically required to cover potential damages or unpaid rent. The deposit is returned to the tenant at the end of the lease, provided the property is in good condition.

- **Utilities:** Responsibilities for paying utilities, such as electricity, water, gas, and internet, should be clearly outlined in the agreement. Some landlords include utilities in the rent amount, while others require tenants to pay them separately.

- **Maintenance and Repairs:** Responsibilities for maintenance and repairs, both routine and emergency, should be specified in the agreement. Landlords are generally responsible for major repairs, while tenants might be responsible for minor repairs or routine maintenance.

- **Termination Procedures:** Procedures for terminating the lease agreement, including notice periods and grounds for termination, should be clearly stated.

Legal Advice: Seeking Professional Guidance

If you have questions or concerns about a rental agreement, seek legal advice from a qualified lawyer specializing in tenancy law to ensure your rights and interests are protected.

Cultural Nuances: Navigating the Bulgarian Property Market

Navigating the Bulgarian property market involves understanding not only the legal and financial aspects but also the cultural nuances that might influence interactions and negotiations.

Building Relationships: Trust and Personal Connections

Building trust and personal connections are important in Bulgarian culture, and this extends to property transactions. Take the time to get to know your real estate agent, landlord, or seller, engage in friendly conversations, and demonstrate your respect for their culture and customs. Building rapport can foster a more positive and productive interaction.

Direct Communication: Clarity and Honesty

Bulgarians value direct and honest communication. Express your needs, preferences, and expectations clearly, without being overly aggressive or confrontational. Direct communication can help avoid misunderstandings and ensure a smoother transaction.

Negotiation: A Common Practice

Negotiation is a common practice in Bulgaria, especially for rental prices and purchase terms. Be prepared to negotiate politely and respectfully, as it's often expected and can result in a more favorable outcome.

Local Customs: Respecting Traditions and Superstitions

Be aware of local customs, traditions, and superstitions that might influence property transactions. For example, some Bulgarians might avoid moving into a property on certain days or during specific periods considered unlucky.

Embracing the Journey: Finding Your Place in Bulgaria

Whether you choose to buy or rent property in Bulgaria, the journey of finding your perfect place is an integral part of the expat experience. Embrace the process, learn about the local market, engage with professionals, and be open to the cultural nuances that make Bulgaria unique. By navigating the legal landscape, planning your finances wisely, and respecting local customs, you can find your dream home and establish a comfortable and fulfilling life in your new Bulgarian haven.

CHAPTER TWENTY-ONE: Healthcare and Insurance: Ensuring Your Well-being in Bulgaria

Relocating to a new country naturally comes with a need to understand the local healthcare system. Bulgaria, despite its reputation for affordable living, might surprise you with its complex and sometimes challenging healthcare landscape. This chapter aims to provide a comprehensive overview of the Bulgarian healthcare system, the types of health insurance available, and essential tips for ensuring your well-being during your stay in the country.

Decoding the Bulgarian Healthcare System: A Two-Tiered Structure

Bulgaria's healthcare system operates on a two-tiered structure, encompassing both public and private sectors. The public system, funded through mandatory health insurance contributions, aims to provide universal healthcare coverage to all Bulgarian citizens and legally residing foreigners. The private sector, while smaller, offers an alternative for those seeking faster access to specialized treatments, shorter waiting times, and a higher level of comfort.

The National Health Insurance Fund (NHIF): The Cornerstone of Public Healthcare

The National Health Insurance Fund (NHIF), the primary institution responsible for managing and financing public healthcare in Bulgaria, collects mandatory health insurance contributions from employed individuals, self-employed persons, and pensioners. These contributions are pooled to cover the costs of medical services for insured individuals.

Health Insurance Card: Your Key to Public Healthcare Access

To access public healthcare services in Bulgaria, you'll need a health insurance card issued by the NHIF. As an expat working in Bulgaria, your employer will usually handle the registration process and deductions for health insurance contributions. Self-employed individuals are responsible for registering with the NHIF and making their contributions directly.

While your health insurance card grants you access to a wide range of medical services, including consultations with general practitioners (GPs), specialists, hospitalization, emergency care, and prescribed medications, it's important to be aware of some limitations:

- **Waiting Lists:** The public healthcare system often involves waiting lists for certain procedures or specialist appointments, which can sometimes be lengthy.

- **Co-payments:** While public healthcare is not entirely free, co-payments might apply for some services or medications.

- **Varying Standards:** The quality of healthcare facilities and services can vary significantly across different regions and hospitals, with some facilities in larger cities offering more modern equipment and specialized services.

Private Health Insurance: Bridging the Gaps in Public Healthcare

Private health insurance is gaining popularity in Bulgaria, providing an alternative to the public system and addressing some of its shortcomings. Private health insurance offers several advantages:

- **Faster Access to Specialized Treatments:** Private clinics and hospitals often have shorter waiting times for specialized treatments and procedures, reducing the time you might have to wait for necessary medical care.

- **Wider Choice of Hospitals and Doctors:** Private health insurance typically allows you to choose from a wider network of hospitals and doctors, providing you with more flexibility and control over your healthcare options.

- **Higher Level of Comfort and Amenities:** Private clinics and hospitals often offer a higher level of comfort and amenities, including private rooms, more personalized attention, and English-speaking staff.

Choosing Private Health Insurance: Navigating the Options

Numerous private health insurance providers operate in Bulgaria, offering a variety of plans and coverage options. The cost of private health insurance premiums varies based on factors like age, health status, the extent of coverage, and the specific provider.

When choosing private health insurance, consider the following:

- **Coverage:** Carefully review the coverage provided by different plans, paying attention to the types of medical services, treatments, and medications covered. Ensure the plan meets your specific healthcare needs and preferences.

- **Network:** Check the provider's network of hospitals and doctors, ensuring it includes facilities and specialists in your area or those you prefer.

- **Premiums:** Compare premiums from different providers, taking into account your budget and the level of coverage offered. Factor in deductibles, co-payments, and any out-of-pocket expenses that might apply.

- **Reputation:** Research the provider's reputation, customer service, and claims processing procedures to ensure a smooth and reliable experience.

- **Exclusions:** Pay attention to any exclusions or limitations in the policy, such as pre-existing conditions or specific treatments that might not be covered.

Ensuring Your Well-being: Essential Tips for Expats

Navigating the Bulgarian healthcare system and ensuring your well-being requires a proactive approach, awareness of potential challenges, and a willingness to seek assistance when needed. Here are some essential tips for expats:

Register with the NHIF: Securing Your Access to Public Healthcare

Registering with the NHIF is essential for accessing public healthcare services, even if you have private health insurance. Your NHIF card serves as proof of insurance and allows you to receive subsidized medical care at public hospitals and clinics. Your employer will usually handle the registration process for you if you're employed.

Keep Your European Health Insurance Card (EHIC): Access to Emergency Care in EU Countries

If you're an EU citizen, keep your European Health Insurance Card (EHIC) with you at all times. The EHIC provides access to state-provided healthcare in other EU countries on a temporary basis, in case of illness or injury during your travels.

Obtain Private Health Insurance: Bridging the Gaps and Enhancing Your Options

Consider obtaining private health insurance, even if you're registered with the NHIF, to address potential gaps in public healthcare, such as long waiting times, limited choice of providers, and varying standards of care. Private health insurance can provide you with peace of mind and access to a higher level of healthcare services.

Research Healthcare Facilities and Providers: Finding the Right Fit for Your Needs

Research healthcare facilities and providers in your area, including public hospitals, private clinics, and specialists, to identify those that best meet your needs and preferences. Consider factors like location, reputation, specialization, language capabilities, and the availability of modern equipment and services.

Learn Basic Bulgarian Medical Terms: Facilitating Communication with Healthcare Professionals

While English is spoken in some healthcare facilities, particularly in larger cities and private clinics, learning basic Bulgarian medical terms can be helpful when communicating with healthcare professionals, especially in smaller towns or rural areas. Simple phrases like "I have a headache" (Боли ме глава - Boli me glava), "I need a prescription" (Имам нужда от рецепта - Imam nuzhda ot retsepta), or "Where is the nearest hospital?" (Къде е най-близката болница? - Kŭde e nai-blizkata bolnitsa?) can facilitate communication and ensure you receive the necessary care.

Bring a Bulgarian-Speaking Friend or Interpreter: Bridging Language Barriers

If you're not confident in your Bulgarian language skills, consider bringing a Bulgarian-speaking friend or hiring a professional interpreter to accompany you to medical appointments. They can facilitate communication, ensure you understand your doctor's instructions and diagnoses, and advocate for your needs.

Utilize Translation Apps or Dictionaries: Supporting Communication

Smartphone translation apps and online dictionaries can be useful tools for bridging language gaps in healthcare settings. However, exercise caution when relying solely on machine translations, as they might not always be accurate, especially for complex medical terminology. It's best to use these tools as a supplement to other communication strategies.

Seek Out English-Speaking Doctors or Clinics: Catering to Expats' Needs

In larger cities and tourist areas, you can often find English-speaking doctors or clinics specializing in expat healthcare. Online directories, expat forums, and your embassy or consulate can provide recommendations for English-speaking healthcare providers.

Pack a Basic First-Aid Kit: Preparedness for Minor Ailments

Pack a basic first-aid kit with essential items like bandages, antiseptic wipes, pain relievers, and anti-diarrhea medication to be prepared for minor ailments or injuries. You can purchase these items at pharmacies (аптека - apteka) in Bulgaria.

Stay Informed About Health Risks: Protecting Yourself from Potential Hazards

Stay informed about potential health risks in Bulgaria, such as tick-borne encephalitis, rabies, and waterborne illnesses. Consult your doctor about recommended vaccinations and preventative measures before your trip, and be mindful of food and water safety practices.

Embrace a Healthy Lifestyle: Boosting Your Well-being

Maintaining a healthy lifestyle, including a balanced diet, regular exercise, and sufficient sleep, is crucial for your overall well-being. Embrace the Mediterranean diet, rich in fruits, vegetables, and olive oil, and take advantage of the abundance of fresh produce available in Bulgarian markets. Engage in physical activities you enjoy, whether it's hiking in the mountains, swimming in the Black Sea, or exploring the city on foot.

Stay Connected with Your Embassy or Consulate: Access to Support and Emergency Assistance

Stay connected with your embassy or consulate in Bulgaria, providing them with your contact information and keeping them informed of your whereabouts, especially if you're traveling to remote areas. Your embassy or consulate can provide guidance, support, and emergency assistance in case of a health crisis or other unexpected situations.

Conclusion

Navigating the Bulgarian healthcare system might present challenges, but being proactive, informed, and prepared can empower you to make the best choices for your health and well-being. Understand the two-tiered structure of public and private healthcare, explore health insurance options, research healthcare providers, and embrace a healthy lifestyle to ensure a comfortable and secure experience in your new Bulgarian home.

CHAPTER TWENTY-TWO: Investing in Bulgaria: Business Opportunities and Real Estate

Bulgaria, a nation on the rise within the European Union, presents a unique landscape for savvy investors seeking promising opportunities in both business ventures and real estate. Its strategic location, bridging East and West, combined with a favorable investment climate and a growing economy, makes it an attractive destination for those looking to diversify their portfolios and tap into emerging markets. This chapter explores the potential of investing in Bulgaria, examining the advantages, considerations, and key sectors for business opportunities, as well as the dynamics and prospects of the Bulgarian real estate market.

Bulgaria's Investment Landscape: A Favorable Climate for Growth

Bulgaria's government has actively fostered a favorable investment climate, implementing policies to attract foreign direct investment, streamline administrative processes, and create a stable economic environment. The country's membership in the European Union provides access to a single market of over 500 million consumers and aligns Bulgaria's regulatory framework with EU standards, enhancing investor confidence.

Key Advantages: Attracting Foreign Investment

Several key advantages make Bulgaria an appealing destination for foreign investors:

- **Strategic Location:** Bulgaria's strategic location at the crossroads of Europe and Asia, with access to both the Black Sea and the Danube River, makes it a logistical hub and a gateway to regional markets.

- **EU Membership:** Bulgaria's membership in the European Union provides access to the single market, free movement of goods and services, and a stable legal and regulatory framework, aligning with EU standards.

- **Competitive Labor Costs:** Bulgaria's labor costs are relatively lower than in many Western European countries, offering cost advantages for businesses operating in labor-intensive industries.

- **Skilled Workforce:** Bulgaria boasts a well-educated and skilled workforce, particularly in sectors like information technology (IT), engineering, and manufacturing, providing a pool of talent for businesses seeking qualified employees.

- **Government Incentives:** The Bulgarian government offers various incentives for foreign investors, including tax breaks, subsidies, and support for research and development activities, encouraging investment in key sectors and promoting economic growth.

- **Growing Economy:** Bulgaria's economy has been growing steadily in recent years, driven by sectors like IT, tourism, manufacturing, and agriculture, creating opportunities for business expansion and investment.

- **Low Corporate Tax Rate:** Bulgaria has a flat corporate tax rate of 10%, one of the lowest in the European Union, making it an attractive location for businesses seeking to optimize their tax burdens.

- **Currency Stability:** The Bulgarian lev (BGN) is pegged to the euro (EUR) at a fixed exchange rate, providing stability and predictability for international transactions and reducing currency risk for investors.

Business Opportunities: Exploring Key Sectors

Bulgaria's diverse economy offers a range of business opportunities across various sectors, attracting both local and foreign investors seeking promising ventures and growth potential. Here are some key sectors to consider:

Information Technology (IT): A Thriving Sector with Global Reach

Bulgaria's IT sector has experienced significant growth in recent years, emerging as a regional hub for software development, IT services, and outsourcing, attracting international companies and creating a thriving ecosystem for tech startups and innovation. The sector's success is driven by several factors:

- **Skilled Workforce:** Bulgaria boasts a highly skilled and well-educated workforce in IT, with a strong emphasis on STEM education (science, technology, engineering, and mathematics) and a growing pool of software engineers, developers, and programmers.

- **Competitive Labor Costs:** Bulgaria's labor costs for IT professionals are relatively lower than in many Western European countries, offering cost advantages for companies seeking to outsource or establish development centers.

- **Government Support:** The Bulgarian government actively supports the IT sector, offering incentives, promoting innovation, and fostering a favorable environment for tech startups and investment.

- **Strong Infrastructure:** Bulgaria has a well-developed IT infrastructure, with reliable internet connectivity, data centers, and technology parks, supporting the growth and expansion of the sector.

Tourism: Untapped Potential and Diverse Offerings

Bulgaria's tourism sector, with its diverse offerings, from stunning coastlines and picturesque mountains to historical sites and cultural experiences, holds immense untapped potential for investors seeking to capitalize on the country's growing popularity as a tourist destination.

- **Coastal Tourism:** Bulgaria's Black Sea coastline, with its golden sands, azure waters, and bustling resorts, attracts tourists seeking sun, sand, and relaxation. Investment opportunities exist in developing new resorts, upgrading existing facilities, and offering niche tourism experiences, such as eco-tourism, adventure tourism, and cultural tourism.

- **Mountain Tourism:** Bulgaria's majestic mountains, with their hiking trails, ski resorts, and charming villages, attract tourists seeking outdoor adventures, winter sports, and nature escapes. Investment opportunities exist in developing new ski resorts, upgrading existing facilities, and offering adventure tourism experiences, such as hiking, mountain biking, and rock climbing.

- **Cultural Tourism:** Bulgaria's rich history and cultural heritage, with its ancient sites, medieval wonders, and Ottoman legacy, attract tourists seeking cultural experiences and historical explorations. Investment opportunities exist in developing cultural tourism routes, restoring historical sites, and offering guided tours and educational programs.

Manufacturing: A Traditional Sector with Modernization Potential

Bulgaria has a long-standing tradition in manufacturing, particularly in sectors like automotive, electronics, food processing, and textiles. While the sector faces challenges from global competition and the need for modernization, investment opportunities exist in upgrading facilities, implementing new technologies, and developing niche manufacturing capabilities.

- **Automotive Industry:** Bulgaria has become a hub for automotive component manufacturing, attracting investments from international companies seeking cost-effective production facilities and a skilled workforce. Investment opportunities exist in expanding production capacities, implementing new technologies, and developing expertise in electric vehicle components.

- **Electronics Industry:** Bulgaria's electronics industry has a tradition in producing consumer electronics, telecommunications equipment, and electronic components. Investment opportunities exist in upgrading facilities, implementing new technologies, and developing expertise in areas like artificial intelligence (AI), Internet of Things (IoT), and robotics.

- **Food Processing Industry:** Bulgaria's agricultural sector provides a strong base for the food processing industry, with opportunities for investment in processing, packaging, and exporting high-quality food products, particularly organic and natural foods.

Agriculture: Leveraging Fertile Lands and EU Support

Bulgaria's fertile lands and favorable climate, combined with its access to EU agricultural subsidies and support programs, create opportunities for investment in agricultural production, processing, and export.

- **Organic Farming:** The demand for organic and natural food products is growing globally, and Bulgaria's agricultural sector has the potential to capitalize on this trend, with investments in organic farming practices, certification, and export.

- **Wine Production:** Bulgaria has a long tradition of winemaking, with diverse grape varietals and favorable terroir for producing high-quality wines. Investment opportunities exist in modernizing wineries, expanding production, and developing export markets for Bulgarian wines.

- **Specialty Crops:** Bulgaria has a suitable climate for cultivating specialty crops, such as lavender, roses, and herbs, used in the production of essential oils, perfumes, and cosmetics. Investment opportunities exist in expanding cultivation, processing, and exporting these high-value crops.

Real Estate: A Dynamic Market with Growth Potential

Bulgaria's real estate market has experienced significant growth in recent years, driven by factors like economic development, tourism expansion, and increasing demand for affordable housing. While the market has slowed down in recent years due to the global economic downturn and rising interest rates, it still offers potential for investors seeking long-term capital appreciation and rental income.

Regional Variations: Sofia, Plovdiv, and Coastal Resorts

The Bulgarian real estate market exhibits regional variations, with prices and demand fluctuating based on location, infrastructure, and economic activity.

- **Sofia:** Sofia, as the capital city, generally commands the highest property prices in Bulgaria, particularly for apartments in the city center and houses in desirable neighborhoods. Sofia's growing economy, expanding business sector, and cultural attractions continue to drive demand for both residential and commercial property.

- **Plovdiv:** Plovdiv, Bulgaria's second-largest city and a European Capital of Culture in 2019, has experienced significant growth in its real estate market, with rising property prices and increasing demand for apartments, houses, and commercial spaces. Plovdiv's charming atmosphere, historical attractions, and growing business sector attract both local and foreign investors.

- **Coastal Resorts:** Bulgaria's Black Sea coast, particularly popular resorts like Sunny Beach, Golden Sands, and Sozopol, attracts significant investment in holiday apartments, vacation homes, and tourist facilities. The coastal real estate market is seasonal, with prices and demand fluctuating based on tourist seasons and economic conditions.

Investment Considerations: Due Diligence and Market Trends

Investing in Bulgarian real estate requires careful consideration, due diligence, and an understanding of market trends.

- **Location:** Location is a crucial factor in real estate investment, influencing property prices, rental potential, and capital appreciation. Research different regions, neighborhoods, and property types to identify areas with strong growth potential, good infrastructure, and attractive amenities.

- **Property Type:** The type of property you choose, whether it's an apartment, house, villa, or commercial space, should align with your investment goals, budget, and risk tolerance. Consider factors like rental demand, maintenance costs, and potential for capital appreciation.

- **Market Trends:** Research market trends, including property price fluctuations, rental yields, and economic indicators, to understand the current state of the market and make informed investment decisions.

- **Legal Expertise:** Engage a qualified lawyer specializing in real estate law to assist with due diligence, contract negotiations, and the property purchase process, ensuring your rights and interests are protected.

186

- **Property Management:** If you're purchasing property for rental income, consider engaging a property management company to handle tenant relations, maintenance, and other aspects of property management, allowing you to focus on your investment strategy.

Investment Tips: Navigating the Opportunities

Investing in Bulgaria, whether in business ventures or real estate, presents a unique set of opportunities and considerations. Here are some tips to navigate the investment landscape effectively:

Research and Due Diligence: Understanding the Market

Thorough research and due diligence are crucial for any investment decision. Understand the market dynamics, regulations, and potential risks associated with your chosen sector or investment strategy.

- **Market Research:** Research market trends, economic indicators, and industry analyses to gain insights into the current state and future prospects of your chosen sector.

- **Regulatory Framework:** Familiarize yourself with Bulgaria's legal and regulatory framework for foreign investment, including tax regulations, labor laws, and property ownership rights.

- **Risk Assessment:** Assess potential risks associated with your investment, including market volatility, economic downturns, and political instability. Diversify your portfolio to mitigate risks and spread your investments across different sectors or asset classes.

Local Expertise: Partnerships and Professional Guidance

Leveraging local expertise can be invaluable when investing in Bulgaria. Consider partnering with local businesses, engaging professional consultants, or seeking guidance from industry experts to navigate the local market effectively.

- **Local Partnerships:** Partnering with local businesses can provide access to market knowledge, distribution networks, and valuable insights into local customs and practices.

- **Professional Consultants:** Engage professional consultants, such as lawyers, accountants, and financial advisors, to assist with legal matters, financial planning, and due diligence.

- **Industry Experts:** Seek guidance from industry experts, such as chambers of commerce, trade associations, and investment promotion agencies, to gain insights into specific sectors and identify potential opportunities.

Cultural Sensitivity: Building Trust and Understanding

Cultural sensitivity and awareness of local customs can enhance your interactions and build trust with potential partners, clients, or employees.

- **Language Skills:** Learning Bulgarian, even just the basics, can demonstrate respect for the local culture and facilitate communication.

- **Local Customs:** Be mindful of local customs and etiquette, such as addressing people with formal titles and surnames, respecting personal space, and adhering to social norms.

- **Building Relationships:** Invest time in building relationships with potential partners, clients, or employees, demonstrating your commitment and understanding of the local culture.

Long-Term Perspective: Patience and Persistence

Investing in Bulgaria often requires a long-term perspective, patience, and persistence. The country's economy and investment climate are evolving, and realizing returns on your investment might take time.

- **Long-Term Goals:** Define your long-term investment goals and choose investment strategies that align with your timeframe and risk tolerance.

- **Patience and Flexibility:** Be patient and flexible, adapting your strategies as the market evolves and overcoming challenges that might arise.

- **Persistence and Commitment:** Maintain your commitment to your investment goals, even during periods of market volatility or economic uncertainty.

Monitoring and Evaluation: Tracking Your Investments

Regular monitoring and evaluation of your investments are essential for ensuring they remain aligned with your goals and adjusting your strategies as needed.

- **Performance Tracking:** Track the performance of your investments, including returns, growth, and any fluctuations in value.

- **Market Analysis:** Stay informed about market trends, economic indicators, and industry developments that might impact your investments.

- **Strategy Adjustments:** Be prepared to adjust your investment strategies based on market conditions, performance, and your evolving financial goals.

Conclusion

Bulgaria's investment landscape, with its favorable climate for growth, diverse business opportunities, and dynamic real estate market, presents a promising destination for investors seeking to diversify their portfolios, tap into emerging markets, and capitalize on the country's economic potential. Thorough research, local expertise, cultural sensitivity, and a long-term perspective are crucial for navigating the opportunities and realizing the potential of investing in Bulgaria.

CHAPTER TWENTY-THREE: Retirement in Bulgaria: A Peaceful and Affordable Option

Bulgaria, a land of captivating beauty, rich history, and warm hospitality, has emerged as an increasingly popular destination for retirees seeking a peaceful and affordable retirement haven. The country's idyllic countryside, charming towns, affordable cost of living, and welcoming atmosphere offer a unique blend of tranquility, cultural immersion, and a fulfilling lifestyle for those seeking a serene and enriching retirement experience. This chapter explores the allure of retiring in Bulgaria, examining the advantages, considerations, and practical aspects of making this Balkan gem your retirement destination.

The Allure of Retiring in Bulgaria: A Blend of Tranquility and Affordability

Bulgaria's appeal as a retirement destination stems from a unique combination of factors:

- **Affordable Cost of Living:** One of the most significant advantages of retiring in Bulgaria is its remarkably affordable cost of living compared to many Western European countries. Housing, utilities, groceries, transportation, and healthcare are generally significantly lower, allowing retirees to stretch their pensions further and enjoy a comfortable lifestyle without breaking the bank.

- **Peaceful and Tranquil Environment:** Bulgaria's idyllic countryside, with its rolling hills, verdant valleys, and charming villages, offers a peaceful and tranquil environment, far removed from the hustle and bustle of city life. The slower pace of life, fresh air, and connection to nature create a serene and relaxing atmosphere, conducive to a fulfilling retirement.

191

- **Warm Hospitality and Welcoming Culture:** Bulgarians are renowned for their warm hospitality and welcoming nature, making retirees feel at home and fostering a sense of community. The genuine friendliness and helpfulness of the locals create a supportive and inclusive environment for newcomers.

- **Rich History and Cultural Heritage:** Bulgaria's rich history and cultural heritage, spanning millennia, offer endless opportunities for exploration and discovery. From ancient Thracian tombs and Roman ruins to medieval monasteries and Ottoman-era architecture, Bulgaria's historical treasures provide insights into the country's fascinating past and its cultural influences.

- **Delicious Cuisine and Local Flavors:** Bulgarian cuisine, with its emphasis on fresh, seasonal ingredients, hearty dishes, and local flavors, is a culinary delight for retirees seeking a taste of authentic Bulgarian traditions. Open-air markets (pazars) offer an abundance of fresh produce, local cheeses, and meats, while traditional Bulgarian restaurants (mehanas) serve hearty stews, grilled meats, and savory pastries.

- **Pleasant Climate with Four Distinct Seasons:** Bulgaria experiences four distinct seasons, offering a variety of weather conditions and opportunities for outdoor activities throughout the year. From sunny summers ideal for swimming in the Black Sea to snowy winters perfect for skiing in the mountains, Bulgaria's climate caters to diverse preferences and allows retirees to enjoy a range of outdoor pursuits.

- **Accessible Healthcare System:** Bulgaria has a public healthcare system that provides universal coverage to all Bulgarian citizens and legally residing foreigners, including retirees. While the quality of healthcare facilities and services can vary across different regions, retirees can access affordable medical care through the National Health

Insurance Fund (NHIF). Private healthcare options are also available for those seeking faster access to specialized treatments, shorter waiting times, and a higher level of comfort.

Choosing Your Retirement Haven: Exploring Bulgaria's Regions

Bulgaria offers a diverse range of regions, each with its unique charm, atmosphere, and lifestyle, catering to various preferences and retirement aspirations. Consider the following factors when choosing your retirement haven:

Sofia: The Cosmopolitan Capital with Urban Amenities

Sofia, Bulgaria's capital city, offers a blend of cosmopolitan amenities, cultural attractions, and historical landmarks, appealing to retirees seeking a vibrant urban environment with access to a wide range of services, entertainment, and cultural experiences. However, Sofia's cost of living is generally higher than in other parts of Bulgaria, particularly for housing.

Plovdiv: Affordable Charm in a Cultural Hub

Plovdiv, Bulgaria's second-largest city and a European Capital of Culture in 2019, offers a more affordable cost of living than Sofia, while still providing a vibrant cultural scene, historical attractions, and a charming atmosphere. Plovdiv's Kapana District, with its cobblestone streets, traditional houses, and artistic vibe, is a particularly appealing area for retirees seeking a blend of history, culture, and a lively social scene.

Varna: Coastal Living with Seasonal Charm

Varna, Bulgaria's largest city on the Black Sea coast, offers a coastal lifestyle with access to beautiful beaches, seafront promenades, and a vibrant summer atmosphere. However, Varna's cost of living can fluctuate seasonally, with higher prices during the summer months due to the influx of tourists.

Coastal Resorts: Sun, Sand, and a Relaxed Pace

Bulgaria's coastal resorts, particularly Sunny Beach, Golden Sands, and Sozopol, attract retirees seeking a relaxed pace of life, access to beaches, and a variety of amenities and entertainment options. However, these resorts can become crowded during peak season, and prices for accommodations and dining might be higher.

Mountain Towns: Tranquility, Nature, and Fresh Air

Bulgaria's mountain towns, nestled amidst picturesque landscapes, offer a tranquil environment, fresh air, and opportunities for outdoor activities, appealing to retirees seeking a nature-oriented lifestyle. These towns often have a slower pace of life, a strong sense of community, and lower cost of living compared to larger cities or coastal resorts.

Rural Villages: Authentic Charm and a Connection to Nature

Bulgaria's rural villages, with their traditional houses, cobblestone streets, and a connection to nature, offer an authentic Bulgarian experience, a slower pace of life, and a strong sense of community. The cost of living in rural villages is generally the lowest in Bulgaria, making it an attractive option for retirees seeking a budget-friendly retirement.

Visa and Residency: Securing Your Stay in Bulgaria

To retire in Bulgaria, you'll need to secure the necessary visa and residency permits, ensuring your legal stay in the country and access to various services and rights. The specific requirements and procedures vary depending on your nationality and individual circumstances.

EU Citizens: Freedom of Movement and Residency

Citizens of EU countries enjoy freedom of movement and residency within the European Union, allowing them to retire in Bulgaria without the need for a visa. However, EU citizens residing in Bulgaria for more than three months are required to register their stay with the local municipality, obtaining a residency certificate that confirms their legal residency status.

Non-EU Citizens: Visas and Residence Permits

Non-EU citizens seeking to retire in Bulgaria will need to obtain a long-term visa or residence permit. Bulgaria offers various types of visas and permits, each with specific requirements and eligibility criteria, catering to different purposes and circumstances.

- **Long-Term Residence Permit (Type D Visa):** The Long-Term Residence Permit, often referred to as the Type D Visa, allows non-EU citizens to reside in Bulgaria for an extended period, typically one year, with the possibility of renewal. This permit is often the first step for retirees seeking to establish residency in Bulgaria. To obtain a Long-Term Residence Permit, you'll need to demonstrate sufficient financial means to support yourself during your stay, have valid health insurance, and meet other specific requirements.

- **Pensioner D Visa:** Bulgaria offers a specific visa category for pensioners, the Pensioner D Visa, allowing retirees with a stable pension income to reside in the country. To obtain this visa, you'll need to provide proof of your pension income, demonstrate sufficient financial means to cover your living expenses, have valid health insurance, and meet other specific requirements.

- **Permanent Residence:** After five years of continuous legal residence in Bulgaria with a long-term residence permit, you become eligible to apply for permanent residence. Permanent residence grants you indefinite permission to live and work in Bulgaria, offering greater stability and security.

Seeking Professional Assistance: Navigating the Bureaucracy

The visa and residency application processes can be complex and time-consuming, requiring meticulous attention to detail and adherence to specific regulations. Seeking professional assistance from immigration lawyers or consultants specializing in Bulgarian immigration law can streamline the process, ensure your applications meet all the requirements, and increase your chances of a successful outcome.

Financial Considerations: Managing Your Retirement Finances

Managing your finances wisely is crucial for a comfortable and financially sustainable retirement in Bulgaria. Understanding the local currency, banking system, and tax implications can help you make informed financial decisions and optimize your retirement income.

The Bulgarian Lev (BGN): Understanding the Currency

Bulgaria's official currency is the Bulgarian lev (BGN), denoted by the symbol "лв." The lev is subdivided into 100 stotinki (ст.), although stotinki coins are rarely used in everyday transactions due to their low value. The lev has been pegged to the euro (EUR) at a fixed exchange rate of 1.95583 leva per euro since 1999. This peg provides stability and predictability for international transactions and makes it relatively easy to calculate the approximate value of goods and services in euros.

The Bulgarian Banking System: Managing Your Finances

Bulgaria's banking system is well-developed and stable, with a network of commercial banks offering a range of financial services, including current accounts, savings accounts, loans, credit cards, and money transfers. The banking sector is supervised by the Bulgarian National Bank (BNB), which ensures the stability and integrity of the financial system.

When choosing a bank in Bulgaria, consider factors like convenience, fees and charges, customer service, and the availability of English-language support. Most banks offer online and mobile banking services, providing 24/7 access to your accounts.

Tax Implications: Understanding Your Obligations

As a retiree in Bulgaria, you might be liable for taxes on your pension income, depending on your residency status and the source of your income. Bulgaria has a flat income tax rate of 10%, applied to all types of income, including pensions. However, double taxation treaties between Bulgaria and other countries might exempt or reduce your tax liability in Bulgaria if you're already paying taxes on your pension income in your home country.

Seeking professional advice from a tax consultant specializing in Bulgarian tax law can help you understand your tax obligations, optimize your tax situation, and ensure compliance with Bulgarian regulations.

Healthcare: Ensuring Your Well-being in Retirement

Healthcare is a crucial consideration for retirees, and Bulgaria offers both public and private healthcare options to ensure your well-being.

The National Health Insurance Fund (NHIF): Accessing Public Healthcare

As a legal resident of Bulgaria, you're eligible to register with the NHIF and access public healthcare services. The NHIF provides universal coverage to all Bulgarian citizens and legally residing foreigners, including retirees. To register with the NHIF, you'll need to provide proof of residency, a valid passport or ID card, and, for non-EU citizens, your residence permit.

While the NHIF covers a wide range of medical services, including consultations with GPs, specialists, hospitalization, emergency care, and prescribed medications, it's important to be aware of potential limitations, such as waiting lists for certain procedures, co-payments for some services, and varying standards of care across different regions and hospitals.

Private Health Insurance: Enhancing Your Healthcare Options

Private health insurance is gaining popularity in Bulgaria, offering an alternative to the public system and addressing some of its shortcomings. Private health insurance provides several advantages:

- **Faster Access to Specialized Treatments:** Private clinics and hospitals often have shorter waiting times for specialized treatments and procedures.

- **Wider Choice of Hospitals and Doctors:** Private health insurance typically allows you to choose from a wider network of hospitals and doctors.

- **Higher Level of Comfort and Amenities:** Private clinics and hospitals often offer a higher level of comfort and amenities, including private rooms, more personalized attention, and English-speaking staff.

Numerous private health insurance providers operate in Bulgaria, offering a variety of plans and coverage options. The cost of private health insurance premiums varies based on factors like age, health status, the extent of coverage, and the specific provider.

When choosing private health insurance, consider the coverage, network, premiums, reputation, and exclusions of different plans to ensure they align with your healthcare needs, preferences, and budget.

Long-Term Care: Planning for Future Needs

As you age, you might require long-term care services, such as assistance with daily activities, nursing care, or specialized medical care. Bulgaria offers both public and private long-term care options.

- **Public Long-Term Care:** Bulgaria's public long-term care system provides subsidized services for eligible individuals, including those with disabilities, chronic illnesses, or age-related health conditions. However, public long-term care facilities might have limited availability, waiting lists, and varying standards of care.

- **Private Long-Term Care:** Private long-term care facilities offer a higher level of comfort, personalized care, and more choices in terms of location and services. However, private long-term care can be expensive, and retirees should carefully consider their financial resources and long-term care needs when planning for their retirement.

Social Life and Integration: Embracing the Bulgarian Experience

Retiring in a new country involves adapting to a new culture, building a social life, and finding ways to integrate into your new community. Bulgaria, with its warm hospitality and welcoming atmosphere, offers a supportive environment for retirees seeking to make new friends, learn the language, and experience the local culture.

Language Learning: Bridging Communication Gaps

Learning Bulgarian, even just the basics, can enhance your social interactions, facilitate communication with locals, and demonstrate your respect for Bulgarian culture. Numerous language schools, private tutors, and online resources offer Bulgarian language courses for all levels, from beginners to advanced learners.

Expat Communities: Connecting with Fellow Expats

Bulgaria has a growing expat community, offering a support network for newcomers, opportunities for social interaction, and a sense of camaraderie. Expat communities often organize social gatherings, cultural events, and information-sharing sessions, helping retirees connect with others, share experiences, and navigate the challenges of settling into a new country.

Local Activities and Interests: Finding Your Passions

Bulgaria offers a wide range of activities and interests to explore, catering to diverse preferences and passions. From hiking in the mountains and swimming in the Black Sea to exploring historical sites and attending cultural events, Bulgaria provides ample opportunities for retirees to stay active, pursue their interests, and make new friends.

Volunteering: Giving Back and Connecting with the Community

Volunteering for local organizations or charities is a rewarding way to give back to your new community, meet like-minded individuals, and make a meaningful contribution. Bulgaria has numerous volunteer opportunities, ranging from assisting with social programs and environmental initiatives to supporting cultural organizations and educational projects.

Practical Considerations: Preparing for Your Retirement Move

Retiring in Bulgaria involves various practical considerations, ensuring a smooth transition and a comfortable settlement in your new home.

Housing: Finding Your Retirement Abode

Bulgaria offers a wide range of housing options, from apartments and houses to villas and rural properties, catering to various budgets and preferences. Consider factors like location, size, amenities, proximity to services, and your desired lifestyle when choosing your retirement abode.

Transportation: Getting Around Bulgaria

Bulgaria has a comprehensive public transportation system, encompassing buses, trains, trams, and trolleybuses, connecting cities, towns, and villages across the country. Public transport is generally affordable and reliable, providing a cost-effective option for retirees seeking to get around without owning a car. Taxis are also relatively affordable, but ensure they use a working meter and agree on the fare beforehand to avoid potential scams or overcharging.

If you plan to drive in Bulgaria, you'll need to obtain a Bulgarian driver's license, either by exchanging your existing foreign driver's license or by taking driving lessons and passing the Bulgarian driving test. Car ownership involves additional costs, such as car insurance, road tax, fuel, and maintenance.

Bringing Your Belongings: Shipping or Relocating

If you're planning to relocate your belongings to Bulgaria, consider the costs and logistics of shipping or hiring a moving company. Research different shipping options, compare quotes, and ensure your belongings are properly insured during transit.

Pets: Relocating with Your Furry Companions

If you're planning to retire in Bulgaria with your pets, research the requirements and procedures for bringing animals into the country. Bulgaria requires pets to have a microchip, rabies vaccination, and other health certificates. Airlines and pet relocation companies can assist with the logistics of transporting your pets safely and comfortably.

Cultural Adaptation: Embracing a New Way of Life

Retiring in a new country involves adapting to a new culture, embracing different customs, and navigating potential cultural differences. Bulgaria, with its unique traditions, social norms, and communication styles, might present challenges for retirees unfamiliar with the local culture. Approach these differences with an open mind, a willingness to learn, and a sense of humor. Engage with locals, ask questions, and embrace the opportunity to experience a new way of life.

Retiring in Bulgaria: A Fulfilling Chapter in Your Life

Retiring in Bulgaria offers a unique opportunity to embrace a new chapter in your life, filled with tranquility, cultural immersion, and a fulfilling lifestyle. The country's affordable cost of living, peaceful environment, warm hospitality, and diverse opportunities for exploration and social engagement create a welcoming haven for retirees seeking a serene and enriching retirement experience. By carefully considering the practical aspects, navigating the legal and financial considerations, and embracing the local culture, you can make Bulgaria your retirement destination and enjoy the rewards of a peaceful and enriching life in this captivating Balkan gem.

CHAPTER TWENTY-FOUR: Bulgarian Legal System: Understanding Laws and Regulations

Moving to a new country involves adapting to a new set of laws and regulations. Bulgaria, with its civil law system and its membership in the European Union, has a legal framework that reflects both its national heritage and its adherence to EU standards. This chapter provides an overview of the Bulgarian legal system, highlighting key aspects that expats should be aware of, from the Constitution and the court system to criminal law, civil law, and administrative regulations. Understanding these legal fundamentals can empower you to navigate your new environment with confidence and ensure your actions align with Bulgarian law.

The Bulgarian Constitution: The Foundation of the Legal System

The Bulgarian Constitution, adopted in 1991, is the supreme law of the land, establishing the country's political system, fundamental rights and freedoms, and the framework for the legal system. The Constitution guarantees basic rights, including:

- **Right to Life, Liberty, and Security:** The Constitution protects the right to life, liberty, and security of person, prohibiting torture, inhuman or degrading treatment, and arbitrary detention.

- **Freedom of Expression, Assembly, and Association:** The Constitution guarantees freedom of expression, assembly, and association, allowing individuals to express their opinions, gather peacefully, and form organizations to pursue common interests.

- **Right to Property:** The Constitution protects the right to private property, allowing individuals to own, use, sell, and inherit property. However, certain restrictions apply to foreign ownership of land, particularly agricultural land.

- **Right to Education, Healthcare, and Social Security:** The Constitution recognizes the right to education, healthcare, and social security, providing a framework for the state to ensure these essential services for its citizens and legal residents.

- **Equality Before the Law:** The Constitution guarantees equality before the law, prohibiting discrimination based on race, ethnicity, gender, religion, or social status.

- **Right to a Fair Trial:** The Constitution guarantees the right to a fair trial, ensuring due process, the presumption of innocence, and the right to legal representation.

The Bulgarian Court System: Ensuring Justice and Upholding the Law

Bulgaria's court system, a crucial component of its legal framework, ensures justice, upholds the law, and provides a mechanism for resolving disputes and adjudicating legal matters. The court system is hierarchical, with different levels of courts handling cases based on their severity, complexity, and subject matter.

Regional Courts (Районни съдилища): The First Instance

Regional courts, the first instance in the Bulgarian court system, handle a wide range of civil and criminal cases, including:

- **Civil Cases:** Disputes related to contracts, property, family matters, inheritance, and personal injury.

- **Criminal Cases:** Minor offenses, such as theft, vandalism, and traffic violations.

District Courts (Окръжни съдилища): Appeals and More Serious Cases

District courts handle appeals from regional courts and have original jurisdiction over more serious criminal cases, including:

- **Appeals:** Appeals from decisions of regional courts, reviewing the case and potentially overturning or modifying the original judgment.

- **Serious Criminal Cases:** Cases involving major offenses, such as murder, robbery, and drug trafficking.

Appellate Courts (Апелативни съдилища): Reviewing District Court Decisions

Appellate courts review decisions of district courts, ensuring the law is applied correctly and that due process is followed. Appellate courts do not retry the case but rather examine the legal arguments and evidence presented to the district court, potentially upholding, overturning, or modifying the district court's judgment.

Supreme Court of Cassation (Върховен касационен съд): The Highest Court

The Supreme Court of Cassation, the highest court in Bulgaria, ensures the uniform application of the law across the country. It reviews decisions of lower courts, particularly appellate court decisions, ensuring consistency in legal interpretation and preventing discrepancies in the application of the law. The Supreme Court of Cassation's decisions are final and binding on all lower courts.

Specialized Courts: Addressing Specific Legal Areas

Bulgaria also has specialized courts that handle specific legal areas, including:

- **Administrative Courts:** Handling disputes between individuals and state institutions, such as tax disputes, social security claims, and administrative sanctions.

- **Commercial Courts:** Handling disputes related to commercial law, such as contracts, bankruptcy, and intellectual property.

- **Military Courts:** Handling cases involving military personnel and offenses related to military law.

The Role of Lawyers: Navigating the Legal System

Lawyers play a crucial role in the Bulgarian legal system, providing legal representation, advice, and guidance to individuals and businesses navigating legal matters. Engaging a qualified lawyer specializing in the relevant area of law is essential for protecting your rights, understanding your legal obligations, and ensuring your case is presented effectively in court.

Finding a Lawyer: Resources and Recommendations

To find a lawyer in Bulgaria, you can explore various resources:

- **Bulgarian Bar Association:** The Bulgarian Bar Association (Българска адвокатска колегия), the professional organization for lawyers in Bulgaria, maintains a directory of registered lawyers, allowing you to search for lawyers specializing in specific legal areas.

- **Embassy or Consulate:** Your embassy or consulate might have a list of recommended lawyers or legal service providers in Bulgaria.

- **Expat Communities:** Expat communities and forums often share recommendations for reputable lawyers who have experience working with foreigners.

- **Online Directories:** Online directories, such as legal service websites or business directories, can provide listings of lawyers in Bulgaria.

Legal Fees: Understanding the Costs

Legal fees in Bulgaria can vary depending on the complexity of the case, the lawyer's experience, and the agreed-upon fee structure. Some lawyers charge hourly rates, while others might charge fixed fees for specific services, such as drafting contracts or representing clients in court. Clarify the lawyer's fee structure and payment arrangements before engaging their services.

Criminal Law: Offenses and Penalties

Bulgaria's criminal law system defines offenses and penalties, outlining the legal consequences for individuals who violate criminal statutes. The severity of the offense and the circumstances surrounding it determine the penalties, which can range from fines and community service to imprisonment.

Categories of Offenses: Minor to Serious Crimes

Bulgarian criminal law categorizes offenses into three main categories:

1. **Petty Offenses (Нарушения):** Minor violations, such as traffic violations, littering, and public intoxication, typically punishable by fines.

2. **Misdemeanors (Престъпления):** More serious offenses, such as theft, assault, and vandalism, punishable by fines, community service, or imprisonment up to three years.

3. **Felonies (Тежки престъпления):** Major offenses, such as murder, robbery, drug trafficking, and organized crime, punishable by imprisonment for more than three years, up to life imprisonment in some cases.

Rights of the Accused: Due Process and Legal Representation

The Bulgarian Constitution guarantees the rights of the accused in criminal proceedings, ensuring due process and a fair trial. These rights include:

- **Presumption of Innocence:** Individuals are presumed innocent until proven guilty beyond a reasonable doubt.

- **Right to Silence:** Individuals have the right to remain silent and not incriminate themselves.

- **Right to Legal Representation:** Individuals have the right to legal representation, either hiring a private lawyer or having a court-appointed lawyer if they cannot afford one.

- **Right to a Fair Trial:** Individuals have the right to a fair trial, including the right to confront witnesses, present evidence, and appeal a conviction.

Civil Law: Resolving Disputes and Protecting Rights

Bulgaria's civil law system governs relationships between individuals, businesses, and other entities, addressing a wide range of legal matters, from contracts and property to family law and inheritance.

Contracts: Agreements and Obligations

Contracts, legally binding agreements between two or more parties, are a fundamental aspect of civil law, governing transactions, business relationships, and other interactions. Bulgarian contract law outlines the requirements for valid contracts, the rights and obligations of parties, and remedies for breaches of contract.

Property: Ownership, Use, and Transfer

Property law governs the ownership, use, and transfer of real estate and other assets. Bulgaria's property law system defines different types of ownership, outlines the procedures for buying and selling property, and addresses issues related to inheritance, mortgages, and easements.

Family Law: Marriage, Divorce, and Child Custody

Family law governs legal matters related to marriage, divorce, child custody, and child support. Bulgarian family law defines the requirements for marriage, outlines the procedures for divorce, and establishes the legal framework for determining child custody and support arrangements.

Inheritance: Distributing Assets After Death

Inheritance law governs the distribution of assets after a person's death. Bulgaria's inheritance law system outlines the rules for intestate succession (when a person dies without a will) and testamentary succession (when a person dies with a will), determining how assets are distributed among heirs.

Torts: Civil Wrongs and Liability

Tort law addresses civil wrongs, such as negligence, defamation, and product liability, providing remedies for individuals who have suffered harm or injury due to the actions or omissions of others. Bulgarian tort law outlines the elements of various torts, the standards for proving liability, and the types of damages that can be awarded.

Administrative Law: Regulations and Interactions with State Institutions

Administrative law governs the actions and regulations of state institutions, outlining the procedures for administrative decisions, the rights of individuals in administrative proceedings, and the mechanisms for appealing administrative decisions.

Administrative Procedures: Ensuring Due Process

Administrative procedures, the rules and processes followed by state institutions when making decisions or taking actions, are designed to ensure due process, fairness, and transparency. These procedures typically involve:

- **Notification:** Informing individuals or businesses affected by an administrative decision about the decision and the reasons for it.

- **Opportunity to Respond:** Providing individuals or businesses with an opportunity to respond to the decision, present evidence, and make arguments before a final decision is made.

- **Written Decision:** Issuing a written decision, outlining the reasons for the decision and any legal basis for it.

Appeals: Challenging Administrative Decisions

Individuals or businesses who disagree with an administrative decision can appeal it to a higher administrative authority or to an administrative court. The appeal process allows for a review of the decision, potentially overturning or modifying it if it's found to be unlawful or unfair.

Practical Tips: Navigating the Legal Landscape

Navigating the Bulgarian legal system might seem daunting, but understanding the basic principles, being aware of your rights and obligations, and seeking professional assistance when needed can make the process smoother. Here are some practical tips:

Familiarize Yourself with Basic Laws and Regulations: Awareness is Key

Familiarize yourself with basic laws and regulations related to your daily life, work, and business activities. Government websites, embassy or consulate websites, and legal information portals can provide valuable resources.

Seek Legal Advice: Professional Guidance and Protection

If you're facing a legal issue or have questions about Bulgarian law, seek legal advice from a qualified lawyer specializing in the relevant area of law. A lawyer can provide guidance, protect your rights, and represent you effectively in legal proceedings.

Respect Local Customs and Norms: Avoiding Unintentional Violations

Be aware of local customs and norms, as some behaviors that might be acceptable in other countries could be considered violations of Bulgarian law. For example, public intoxication or disorderly conduct might result in fines or legal action.

Stay Informed: Keeping Up with Legal Changes

Bulgaria's legal framework is constantly evolving, with new laws and regulations being adopted or amended periodically. Stay informed about legal changes that might affect your rights or obligations. Government websites, legal news sources, and professional organizations can provide updates on legal developments.

Utilize Online Resources: Accessing Legal Information

Bulgaria has numerous online resources that provide access to legal information, including:

- **National Assembly of Bulgaria:** The National Assembly's website provides access to the Bulgarian Constitution, laws, and regulations.

- **Ministry of Justice:** The Ministry of Justice's website offers information about the court system, legal procedures, and legal aid services.

- **Bulgarian Bar Association:** The Bulgarian Bar Association's website provides a directory of registered lawyers and information about legal services.

Embrace the Legal Framework: A Foundation for a Secure and Fulfilling Life

Bulgaria's legal system, with its emphasis on due process, the protection of rights, and the resolution of disputes, provides a framework for a secure and fulfilling life in your new Bulgarian home. By understanding the legal fundamentals, seeking professional assistance when needed, and respecting local customs and norms, you can navigate the legal landscape with confidence, ensuring your actions align with Bulgarian law and your rights are protected.

CHAPTER TWENTY-FIVE: Integrating into Bulgarian Society: Embracing a New Way of Life

Moving to a new country, even one as welcoming as Bulgaria, involves adapting to a new culture, navigating social nuances, and finding ways to integrate into your new community. It's a journey of discovery, requiring an open mind, a willingness to embrace differences, and a genuine desire to connect with the people and the place you now call home. This chapter explores the multifaceted aspects of integrating into Bulgarian society, offering insights and practical guidance to help you navigate this transition smoothly and create a fulfilling and enriching life in your new Bulgarian home.

Bridging Cultural Gaps: Understanding Bulgarian Perspectives

Bulgaria's culture, shaped by its rich history, diverse influences, and unique traditions, might present both similarities and differences compared to your own cultural background. Embracing an open-minded and respectful approach to these cultural nuances is crucial for fostering positive interactions and building meaningful connections with Bulgarians.

The Importance of History: A Source of National Pride

Bulgaria's long and storied history, marked by the rise and fall of empires, cultural influences, and periods of both prosperity and hardship, has instilled a deep sense of national pride in its people. Bulgarians often take pride in their country's heritage, its traditions, and its resilience in the face of adversity.

Understanding the significance of history in Bulgarian culture can provide insights into the values, perspectives, and national identity of its people. Engage in conversations about history, show interest in learning about Bulgaria's past, and appreciate the cultural landmarks and traditions that reflect its historical journey.

Family and Community: Strong Bonds and Social Support

Family and community play a central role in Bulgarian culture, with close-knit ties, strong bonds, and a sense of collective responsibility. Extended families often live close to each other, providing support, sharing responsibilities, and celebrating traditions together. Community spirit is also strong, with neighbors often knowing each other, helping each other out, and participating in local events and celebrations.

Direct Communication: Clarity and Honesty

Bulgarian communication style is generally direct and straightforward, with less emphasis on indirect communication or nuanced expressions. Bulgarians value clarity, honesty, and sincerity in their interactions, expressing their thoughts and opinions directly, without beating around the bush.

While this directness might seem blunt at times, it's not intended to be rude or disrespectful. Embrace this directness in your own communication, expressing your thoughts and feelings openly and honestly, while maintaining a respectful and considerate tone.

Nonverbal Communication: Body Language and Gestures

Nonverbal communication, including body language, facial expressions, and gestures, plays a significant role in Bulgarian interactions, often conveying additional meaning beyond spoken words. Pay attention to these nonverbal cues to understand the full context of a conversation and ensure your own nonverbal communication aligns with Bulgarian norms.

- **Eye Contact:** Maintaining eye contact during conversations is a sign of respect and engagement, conveying your interest and attentiveness.

214

- **Head Nod:** A nod of the head can indicate agreement, understanding, or acknowledgment.

- **Hand Gestures:** Bulgarians often use hand gestures to emphasize points, express emotions, or illustrate their words. Familiarize yourself with common Bulgarian gestures to avoid misinterpretations or unintentional offenses.

Humor: A Shared Connection and Cultural Insight

Humor is an integral part of Bulgarian culture, often used to lighten the mood, build rapport, and create a sense of connection. Bulgarian humor can be witty, ironic, or self-deprecating, reflecting the country's history, cultural experiences, and a tendency to find humor even in challenging situations.

Engage in humorous exchanges, share a laugh, and appreciate the cultural nuances of Bulgarian humor. However, be mindful of sensitive topics, cultural differences, and jokes that might be misconstrued or considered offensive.

Superstitions: Folklore and Traditional Beliefs

Bulgarians have a rich tapestry of folklore, traditions, and superstitions, some deeply rooted in ancient beliefs and practices. While not everyone adheres to these superstitions, they are often ingrained in everyday language, customs, and social interactions.

- **The Evil Eye (Уроки):** The belief in the "evil eye," a malevolent gaze that can bring bad luck or misfortune, is prevalent in Bulgarian culture. People often wear amulets, charms, or red strings to ward off the evil eye.

- **Spilling Salt:** Spilling salt is considered bad luck, and it's customary to throw a pinch of salt over your left shoulder to counteract the misfortune.

- **Black Cat Crossing Your Path:** A black cat crossing your path is also considered bad luck. To avoid the misfortune, some people might wait for someone else to cross the path first or spit over their left shoulder.

- **Knocking on Wood:** Knocking on wood, often accompanied by the phrase "да чукна на дърво" (da chukna na dŭrvo), is a common superstition to ward off bad luck or prevent jinxing something good.

Be aware of these superstitions, respect their cultural significance, and avoid actions or words that might be perceived as disrespectful or insensitive to these beliefs.

Building Bridges: Connecting with Bulgarians

Building meaningful connections with Bulgarians is essential for integrating into society, fostering a sense of belonging, and creating a fulfilling social life. While language barriers and cultural differences might present initial challenges, approaching interactions with genuine interest, respect, and a willingness to learn can open doors to meaningful relationships and a deeper understanding of Bulgarian culture.

Language Learning: Unlocking Communication and Cultural Insights

Learning Bulgarian, even just the basics, is a powerful tool for connecting with Bulgarians, demonstrating your commitment to integration, and unlocking deeper cultural insights. While English is spoken in some sectors and tourist areas, fluency in Bulgarian opens doors to more meaningful conversations, a better understanding of cultural nuances, and a deeper appreciation for Bulgarian humor, expressions, and perspectives.

- **Language Schools:** Numerous language schools offer Bulgarian language courses for all levels, from beginners to advanced learners. These courses typically focus on grammar, vocabulary, pronunciation, and conversational skills, providing a structured learning environment and opportunities to practice with other students.

- **Private Tutors:** Private tutors offer personalized language instruction tailored to your individual needs and learning style. They can provide one-on-one lessons, focusing on specific areas, such as grammar, pronunciation, or conversational practice, and accommodating your availability and learning pace.

- **Online Resources:** A wealth of online resources, including websites, apps, and online communities, can support your Bulgarian language learning journey. These resources offer grammar lessons, vocabulary exercises, pronunciation guides, and opportunities for language exchange with native speakers.

- **Immersion and Daily Practice:** The key to language fluency is immersion and daily practice. Engage with the language in everyday life, even if it's just a few words or phrases at a time. Watch Bulgarian movies and TV shows, listen to Bulgarian music, read Bulgarian books and newspapers, and practice speaking with locals whenever possible.

Expat Communities: Support Networks and Shared Experiences

Connecting with other expats can provide a valuable support network during your initial adjustment to life in Bulgaria, offering shared experiences, practical advice, and a sense of camaraderie. Expat communities often organize social gatherings, events, and activities, creating opportunities to meet like-minded individuals, exchange information, and navigate the challenges of settling into a new country.

- **Online Forums and Groups:** Online forums and groups dedicated to expats in Bulgaria offer a virtual space to connect with others, seek advice, and share experiences.

These platforms often feature discussions on various topics, from visa and residency issues to finding housing, schools, and healthcare providers.

- **Social Media Groups:** Social media groups, particularly Facebook groups, are a popular way for expats to connect locally, discover events, and share information. Many towns and cities have dedicated expat groups, featuring posts about upcoming events, social gatherings, recommendations for local businesses, and discussions on various aspects of expat life.

- **Expat Organizations and Clubs:** Expat organizations and clubs offer more structured activities and networking opportunities, often organizing events, such as language exchanges, cultural excursions, social gatherings, and charity initiatives. These organizations provide a platform to meet people with shared interests, expand your social circle, and contribute to your new community.

Engaging with Locals: Building Bridges through Shared Interests

Engaging with locals through shared interests is a natural and rewarding way to build bridges, foster connections, and gain a deeper understanding of Bulgarian culture and perspectives. Whether it's through hobbies, sports, volunteer work, or cultural activities, these shared experiences create common ground, facilitate communication, and open doors to genuine friendships.

- **Sports Clubs:** Joining a sports club, whether it's football, volleyball, basketball, tennis, or swimming, provides opportunities to stay active, improve your fitness, and connect with people who share your passion for sports. Sports clubs often organize social events and outings, fostering team spirit and camaraderie.

- **Hobby Groups:** Explore hobby groups, such as photography clubs, hiking groups, book clubs, or cooking classes, to connect with people who share your interests and passions. These groups provide a platform to learn new skills, share knowledge, and engage in social activities.

- **Volunteer Organizations:** Volunteering for a local organization, such as a charity, environmental group, or community initiative, offers a rewarding way to give back to your new community, make a meaningful contribution, and connect with people who share your values. Volunteering provides opportunities to meet like-minded individuals, learn about local issues, and contribute to positive change.

- **Cultural Events:** Attend local cultural events, such as festivals, concerts, theater performances, and art exhibitions, to immerse yourself in Bulgarian culture, experience local traditions, and engage in conversations with Bulgarians who share your appreciation for the arts.

- **Language Exchanges:** Participate in language exchanges, where you can practice your Bulgarian with native speakers and help them learn your language in return. Language exchanges offer a fun and interactive way to improve your language skills, gain cultural insights, and make new friends.

Respecting Local Customs: Navigating Social Nuances

Respecting local customs and social norms is crucial for fostering positive interactions and building meaningful relationships with Bulgarians. While Bulgarians are generally warm and welcoming, being aware of cultural differences and adjusting your behavior accordingly demonstrates your respect for their culture and fosters a more harmonious integration.

- **Greetings:** When greeting someone for the first time, it's customary to use formal titles and surnames, unless invited to use more informal terms. Maintain eye contact during greetings, as it conveys respect and engagement. A handshake is the most common form of greeting.

- **Personal Space:** Bulgarians tend to stand a bit closer during conversations than in some other cultures. Don't be alarmed if someone stands closer than you're accustomed to; it's not intended to be intrusive but rather reflects a cultural difference in personal space.

- **Gift-Giving:** Gift-giving is a common practice in Bulgaria, expressing appreciation, gratitude, or celebrating special occasions. When choosing a gift, consider the recipient's interests, preferences, and the occasion. Avoid giving expensive or extravagant gifts, as it might make the recipient feel uncomfortable. A small, thoughtful gift, such as flowers, chocolates, or a local souvenir, is usually appreciated.

- **Dining Etiquette:** Bulgarian table manners reflect a culture that values politeness and respect. Wait for the host to invite you to sit before taking your place at the table. Use utensils for most meals, keep your hands above the table, and avoid starting to eat until everyone is served. Compliment the host on the food and finish everything on your plate as a sign of appreciation.

- **Alcohol Consumption:** Alcohol, particularly rakia, a traditional fruit brandy, plays a role in Bulgarian social gatherings. However, excessive drinking is generally frowned upon, and moderation is key. Toasting is a common tradition, and it's customary to look into the eyes of the person you're toasting with and say "Наздраве!" (Nazdrave!), meaning "Cheers!"

Patience and Understanding: Embracing the Journey of Integration

Integrating into Bulgarian society is a gradual process that takes time, patience, and a willingness to embrace both the joys and challenges of adapting to a new culture. Be patient with yourself, celebrate your successes, and don't be discouraged by occasional setbacks or misunderstandings. Embrace the journey, and you'll find that integrating into Bulgarian society can be a rewarding and enriching experience.

Overcoming Challenges: Navigating Potential Obstacles

While Bulgaria is generally a welcoming country for expats, integrating into society might present challenges that require patience, understanding, and a proactive approach to overcome.

Language Barrier: A Common Hurdle

The language barrier can be a significant obstacle for expats, especially in the initial stages of settling into Bulgaria. While English is spoken in some sectors and tourist areas, fluency in Bulgarian is often essential for navigating everyday life, accessing services, and building deeper connections with locals. Commit to learning Bulgarian, embrace opportunities to practice, and don't be afraid to make mistakes. Persistence and a positive attitude can help you overcome the language barrier and unlock the richness of Bulgarian culture and communication.

Cultural Differences: Navigating Misunderstandings

Cultural differences, particularly in communication styles, social norms, and values, can lead to misunderstandings or social faux pas. Be mindful of these differences, observe how Bulgarians interact, and ask questions to clarify any uncertainties. Embrace an open-minded and respectful approach, recognizing that these differences enrich the cultural experience and provide opportunities for learning and growth.

Bureaucracy: Navigating Administrative Processes

Bulgaria's bureaucracy, while often perceived as complex and time-consuming, is an unavoidable aspect of life in the country.

Understanding the system, gathering the necessary documents in advance, being patient and persistent, and seeking assistance from professionals or Bulgarian-speaking friends can help you navigate administrative processes more effectively and minimize potential frustrations.

Finding Employment: Competition and Language Requirements

Finding employment in Bulgaria can be challenging, especially for expats who are not fluent in Bulgarian or lack specialized skills in high-demand sectors. Competition for jobs can be high, and many positions require proficiency in Bulgarian. Research the job market, develop your language skills, network with professionals, and consider seeking assistance from recruitment agencies to enhance your job prospects.

Homesickness: Adjusting to a New Environment

Homesickness is a common experience for expats, especially in the initial stages of settling into a new country. Maintaining connections with family and friends back home, creating a comfortable living space, engaging in familiar activities, and exploring your new surroundings can help alleviate feelings of homesickness and foster a sense of belonging in your new environment.

Embracing the Bulgarian Experience: A Journey of Growth and Discovery

Integrating into Bulgarian society is not just about adapting to a new culture; it's about embracing the opportunities for growth, discovery, and personal enrichment that come with living in a new environment. Embrace the challenges, celebrate the triumphs, and allow yourself to be transformed by the experiences that shape your journey.

Building a Life in Bulgaria: A Mosaic of Experiences

Integrating into Bulgarian society is a multifaceted and ongoing process, involving a mosaic of experiences, interactions, and personal reflections. Embrace the journey, learn from the challenges, celebrate the successes, and allow yourself to be transformed by the richness of Bulgarian culture and the warmth of its people. By approaching integration with an open mind, a respectful heart, and a willingness to learn and grow, you can create a fulfilling and enriching life in your new Bulgarian home.

Printed in Great Britain
by Amazon

53455052R00123